Jesus Christ — the Life of the World
Jésus Christ, vie du monde
Jesus Christus, das Leben der Welt
Jesucristo, Vida del Mundo

A **worship book** for the Sixth Assembly
of the World Council of Churches

Louanges et prières *à l'usage de la Sixième Assemblée
du Conseil œcuménique des Eglises*

Ein **Gottesdienstbuch** für die Sechste Vollversammlung
des Ökumenischen Rates der Kirchen

Libro de Culto *para la Sexta Asamblea
del Consejo Mundial de Iglesias*

World Council of Churches, Geneva
Conseil œcuménique des Eglises, Genève
Ökumenischer Rat der Kirchen, Genf
Consejo Mundial de Iglesias, Ginebra

The cover picture on the theme "Jesus Christ — the Life of the World", based on John 12:24, is by Jyoti Sahi, India.

Le dessin de la couverture sur le thème «Jésus-Christ, vie du monde» s'inspire de Jean 12, 24. Il est de Jyoti Sahi, Inde.

Das Titelbild zum Thema «Jesus Christus, das Leben der Welt», inspiriert von Johannes 12, 24, stammt von Jyoti Sahi, Indien.

El dibujo de la portada, que se refiere al tema «Jesucristo, Vida del Mundo» y está inspirado en Juan 12:24, es de Jyoti Sahi, India.

Music typeset by ISEDET, Buenos Aires

Cover design: Niels Wamberg

IBSN No. 2-8254-0761-5

Printed in Switzerland

This book is dedicated
to the late Doreen Potter (†1980) and Erik Routley (†1982),
whose work, particularly on *Cantate Domino,*
continues to enrich the music and poetry of the oikoumene.

Ce recueil est dédié
à Doreen Potter, décédée en 1980, et à Erik Routley, décédé en 1982,
qui, grâce à la contribution qu'ils ont apportée au Cantate Domino,
continuent d'enrichir la musique et la poésie de l'oikoumene.

Dieses Buch ist dem Andenken
von Doreen Potter (†1980) und Eric Routley (†1982) gewidmet,
deren Werk — insbesondere *Cantate Domino* —
der Musik und der Textdichtung der Ökumene nach wie vor neue Impulse gibt.

Dedicamos este libro
a Doreen Potter (†1980) y a Erik Routley (†1982),
cuyo trabajo, particularmente el relacionado con el himnario Cantate Domino,
sigue enriqueciendo la música y la poesía del oikoumene.

Contents
Table des matières
Inhaltsverzeichnis
Indice

Introduction · *Introduction* · Einführung · *Introducción* vi

Order of daily worship · *Ordre du culte journalier* · Ordnung des täglichen Gottesdienstes · *Orden de culto diario* xii

LIFE, A GIFT OF GOD · *LA VIE, DON DE DIEU* · LEBEN, EIN GESCHENK GOTTES · *LA VIDA, DON DE DIOS* 1

    I. Biblical affirmations · *Affirmations bibliques* · Biblische Leitsätze · *Afirmaciones bíblicas* 3

    II. Scripture passages · *Extraits de l'Ecriture* · Bibelstellen · *Pasajes de la Sagrada Escritura* 3

    III. Responsive readings and litanies · *Répons et litanies* · Responsorien und Litaneien · *Responsorios y letanías* 4

    IV. Prayers · *Prières* · Gebete · *Oraciones* 11

LIFE CONFRONTING AND OVERCOMING DEATH · *LA VIE VICTORIEUSE DE LA MORT* · LEBEN UND TOD: KONFRONTATION UND ÜBERWINDUNG · *LA VIDA HACE FRENTE Y VENCE A LA MUERTE* 19

    I. Biblical affirmations · *Affirmations bibliques* · Biblische Leitsätze · *Afirmaciones bíblicas* 21

    II. Scripture passages · *Extraits de l'Ecriture* · Bibelstellen · *Pasajes de la Sagrada Escritura* 22

    III. Responsive readings and litanies · *Répons et litanies* · Responsorien und Litaneien · *Responsorios y letanías* 22

    IV. Prayers · *Prières* · Gebete · *Oraciones* 34

LIFE IN ITS FULLNESS · *LA VIE DANS SA PLÉNITUDE* · LEBEN IN SEINER GANZEN FÜLLE · *LA VIDA EN SU PLENITUD* 41

    I. Biblical affirmations · *Affirmations bibliques* · Biblische Leitsätze · *Afirmaciones bíblicas* 43

    II. Scripture passages · *Extraits de l'Ecriture* · Bibelstellen · *Pasajes de la Sagrada Escritura* 43

    III. Responsive readings and litanies · *Répons et litanies* · Responsorien und Litaneien · *Responsorios y letanías* 44

    IV. Prayers · *Prières* · Gebete · *Oraciones* 51

LIFE IN UNITY · *LA VIE DANS L'UNITÉ* · LEBEN IN EINHEIT · *LA VIDA EN LA UNIDAD* 61

    I. Biblical affirmations · *Affirmations bibliques* · Biblische Leitsätze · *Afirmaciones bíblicas* 63

    II. Scripture passages · *Extraits de l'Ecriture* · Bibelstellen · *Pasajes de la Sagrada Escritura* 63

    III. Responsive readings and litanies · *Répons et litanies* · Responsorien und Litaneien · *Responsorios y letanías* 64

    IV. Prayers · *Prières* · Gebete · *Oraciones* 71

ACTS OF PENITENCE · *PRIÈRES DE REPENTANCE* · BUSSGEBETE · *ACTOS DE PENITENCIA* 79

CREEDS · *CONFESSIONS DE FOI* · GLAUBENSBEKENNTNISSE · *CREDOS* 83

CONTEMPORARY AFFIRMATIONS OF FAITH · *AFFIRMATIONS CONTEMPORAINES DE LA FOI* · GLAUBENSBEKENNTNISSE DER GEGENWART · *AFIRMACIONES CONTEMPORANEAS DE FE* 90

GENERAL PRAYERS · *PRIÈRES SANS THÈME PRÉCIS* · ALLGEMEINE GEBETE · *ORACIONES VARIAS* 94

    Opening prayers · *Prières d'ouverture* · Eröffnungsgebete · *Oraciones de apertura* 94

    For understanding · *Pour une meilleure compréhension des autres* · Für ein besseres gegenseitiges Verstehen · *Para una mejor comprensión mutua* 97

    For silence · *Pour le recueillement* · Zum Stillewerden · *Meditación* 99

    At the eucharist · *Pour l'eucharistie* · Beim Abendmahl · *En la eucaristía* 100

    Closing prayers · *Prières de clôture* · Schlussgebete · *Oraciones finales* 101

Music · *Musique* · Musik · *Música* 105

Index of first lines · *Répertoire des titres* · Verzeichnis der Liedanfänge · *Lista de títulos* 107

Sources of prayers · *Sources des prières* · Quellenangaben für die Gebete · *Procedencia de las oraciones* 154

Sources of music · *Sources des cantiques et répons* · Quellenangaben für die Musik · *Procedencia de la música* 156

Sources of illustrations · *Sources des illustrations* · Quellenangaben für die Illustrationen · *Procedencia de las ilustraciones* 165

Introduction

"Jesus Christ—the Life of the World" is the theme of the Sixth Assembly of the World Council of Churches which meets in Vancouver, Canada, from 24 July to 10 August 1983.

Some four thousand Christians from all parts of the world will assemble around that theme. In the light of the affirmation that Jesus Christ is the life of the world, they will review the work and witness of the WCC during the last seven years, and they will set guidelines for its future work.

At the heart of the Assembly programme is worship. The study and the discussions and the debate happen within the context of worship. This book has been compiled in the conviction that our worship, both corporate and private, will inform and inspire all our work at the Assembly.

At Vancouver, much of the worship—the praise and thanksgiving, the confession of sins, the intercession on behalf of the whole inhabited earth, the proclamation of the Word and the celebration of the eucharist—is planned to take place in a special tent. A sign of a pilgrim people, the tent reminds us of the image of the incarnation in John's Gospel, that of God in Jesus Christ pitching a tent among and for us and all of God's creation.

On page xii is an order for daily morning worship. Developed at an international, ecumenical workshop in March 1982, its aim is to enable Christians speaking a variety of languages to worship together in unity.

The first part of the book includes biblical material, responsive readings, litanies and prayers which focus on the four Assembly sub-themes. The second part includes a collection of hymns and sung acclamations, also geared to the Assembly theme. These musical offerings are intended as a supplement to *Cantate Domino*, the ecumenical hymnbook published under WCC auspices.

This book reflects the church in its ecumenical richness. It is culturally and confessionally diverse. It contains both traditional and contemporary prayers. Language inclusive of women and men is the norm. The compilers hope the book will help to expand our liturgical horizons, and that the participants will share the hymns and worship forms of Christians from other cultures and traditions.

Though the immediate purpose of the book is its use at the Assembly, it is also offered in the hope that it will enrich the worship life of

God's people everywhere in the years to come. It is in this hope that the Assembly Worship Committee and the WCC staff related to it greet you in the name of Jesus Christ, the Life of the World.

* * *

We regret that limitations of space made it impossible to publish all the liturgical materials in all the working languages of the WCC.

The responses appear in italics. Small capitals indicate that *all* join in the prayer or response.

We are grateful to those who contributed material for the worship book. We acknowledge our thanks to individuals and organizations who have given us permission to use material already published.

The Evangelical Reformed Churches in the Canton of Berne, Switzerland, have provided financial support for the publication of this book, and we are grateful for this thoughtful gesture.

Introduction

«Jésus-Christ, vie du monde» est le thème de la Sixième Assemblée du Conseil œcuménique des Eglises qui se réunit à Vancouver au Canada, du 24 juillet au 10 août 1983. Près de quatre mille chrétiens venus du monde entier se rassembleront autour de ce thème. A la lumière d'une telle affirmation, ils se pencheront sur le témoignage porté par le COE au cours des sept dernières années et sur les activités accomplies, et ils définiront les grandes orientations des activités futures.

Au cœur du programme de l'Assemblée, il y a la célébration. La réflexion et les discussions des participants s'inscrivent dans le contexte de la prière et de l'adoration. L'équipe qui a composé ce recueil l'a fait dans la conviction que nos prières, celles de chacun de nous et de notre Assemblée, inspireront tous nos travaux.

A Vancouver, une grande partie des cultes — louanges et actions de grâces, confession des péchés, intercessions pour toute la terre habitée, proclamation de la parole — auront lieu sous une tente. Signe d'un peuple en pèlerinage, la tente nous rappelle l'image que donne l'Evangile de Jean de l'incarnation: Dieu en Jésus-Christ plantant sa tente parmi nous et pour nous, et pour toute la création.

On trouvera à la page xii le schéma du culte quotidien du matin. Etabli en mars 1982 lors d'un atelier œcuménique international, il a pour but de permettre à des chrétiens de langues différentes de célébrer Dieu ensemble dans l'unité.

La première partie de cet ouvrage se compose de textes bibliques, de répons, de litanies et de prières portant sur les quatre sous-thèmes de l'Assemblée. La deuxième partie est un recueil de cantiques et d'acclamations chantées, en rapport eux aussi avec le thème de l'Assemblée. Ces offrandes musicales sont destinées à compléter le *Cantate Domino*, recueil œcuménique de cantiques paru sous les auspices du COE.

L'ouvrage est à l'image de l'Eglise et de sa richesse œcuménique. Il reflète sa diversité culturelle et confessionnelle. Prières traditionnelles et prières contemporaines s'y côtoient. Le langage utilisé inclut hommes et femmes. L'équipe qui a préparé ce recueil espère qu'il contribuera à élargir les horizons en matière de liturgie et permettra à chacun de découvrir les cantiques et les formes de culte de chrétiens d'autres cultures et traditions.

Bien qu'il ait été conçu avant tout pour être utilisé à l'Assemblée, ses auteurs espèrent aussi qu'il enrichira la vie cultuelle du peuple de Dieu, où qu'il se trouve, dans les années à venir.

C'est dans cet espoir que le Comité des cultes de l'Assemblée et les membres du personnel du COE qui l'ont secondé dans sa tâche vous saluent en Jésus-Christ, vie du monde.

* * *

En raison de l'espace limité dont nous disposions, il ne nous a malheureusement pas été possible de publier l'ensemble des textes liturgiques dans toutes les langues de travail du COE.

Les répons sont en italique. Les lettres majuscules réduites indiquent que *toute* l'assemblée dit la prière ou le répons.

Nous exprimons notre reconnaissance à tous ceux qui ont contribué à ce recueil de louanges et prières. Nous adressons également nos remerciements aux personnes et aux organisations qui nous ont autorisés à utiliser des documents déjà publiés.

Les Eglises évangéliques réformées du Canton de Berne, Suisse, ont apporté leur soutien financier à la publication de cet ouvrage et nous les remercions de leur générosité.

Einführung

«Jesus Christus, das Leben der Welt» lautet das Thema der Sechsten Vollversammlung des Ökumenischen Rates der Kirchen, die vom 24. Juli bis 10. August 1983 in Vancouver, Kanada, stattfinden wird.

Rund viertausend Christen aus aller Welt werden sich dort versammeln, um sich mit diesem Thema zu befassen. Im Licht dieser Aussage, dass Jesus Christus das Leben der Welt ist, werden sie Arbeit und Zeugnis des ÖRK in den vergangenen sieben Jahren überprüfen und Richtlinien für die künftige Arbeit festlegen.

Der Gottesdienst steht im Mittelpunkt des Vollversammlungs-programms. Reflexion und Diskussion geschehen im Kontext des Gottesdienstes. Dieses Buch ist in der Überzeugung zusammen-gestellt worden, dass unser — gemeinsamer und persönlicher — Gottesdienst unsere Arbeit während der Vollversammlung prägen und inspirieren wird.

Ein grosser Teil der Gottesdienste in Vancouver — Lob und Dank; Sündenbekenntnis; Fürbitten für die ganze bewohnte Erde; Verkün-digung des Wortes und Feier des Abendmahls — soll in einem Zelt stattfinden. Dieses Zelt ist ein Zeichen des wandernden Gottesvolkes und eine Erinnerung an das Bild von der Fleischwerdung im Johan-nesevangelium, nach dem Gott in Jesus Christus sein Zelt unter uns, für uns und für seine ganze Schöpfung aufschlägt (s. Joh. 1, 14).

Auf S. xiii finden Sie eine Ordnung für die täglichen Morgengottes-dienste. Sie wurde im Rahmen einer internationalen ökumenischen Gottesdiensttagung im März 1982 erarbeitet und soll es Christen mit vielen verschiedenen Muttersprachen ermöglichen, gemeinsam und in Einheit Gottesdienste zu feiern.

Dieses Buch enthält im ersten Teil Bibeltexte, Responsorien, Litaneien und Gebete zu den vier Unterthemen der Vollversammlung. Im zweiten Teil sind Lieder und gesungene Akklamationen zusammen-gestellt, die sich ebenfalls auf das Vollversammlungsthema beziehen. Dieses musikalische Angebot ist als Ergänzung zum ökumenischen Gesangbuch *Cantate Domino* gedacht, das im Auftrag des Rates veröffentlicht worden ist.

Dieses Gottesdienstbuch spiegelt den ökumenischen Reichtum der Kirche wider. Es schöpft aus unterschiedlichen kulturellen und kon-fessionellen Traditionen. Es enthält sowohl überlieferte als auch moderne Gebete. Es gebraucht eine Sprache, die Frauen und Männer einschliesst. Die für die Zusammenstellung Verantwortlichen hoffen, dass dieses Buch dazu beiträgt, liturgische Horizonte zu erweitern, und dass es Teilnehmerinnen und Teilnehmer anregt, Lieder und Gottesdienstformen aus anderen Kulturen und Traditionen aufzunehmen.

Zwar ist das Gottesdienstbuch hauptsächlich für die Vollversammlung gedacht, doch besteht zugleich die Hoffnung, dass es das gottesdienstliche Leben des Volkes Gottes überall auf Erden in den kommenden Jahren bereichern wird. Mit dieser Hoffnung grüssen Sie der Gottesdienstausschuss und der mit ihm zusammenarbeitende Mitarbeiterstab des ÖRK im Namen Jesu Christi, der das Leben der Welt ist.

* * *

Wir bedauern, dass es aus Platzgründen nicht möglich war, alles liturgische Material in allen Arbeitssprachen des ÖRK zu veröffentlichen.

Wechselgesänge sind kursiv gedruckt. Kleingedruckte Grossbuchstaben bedeuten, dass *alle* in das Gebet oder den Wechselgesang einstimmen.

Wir danken allen, die Material für das Gottesdienstbuch beigetragen haben. Ferner danken wir Einzelpersonen und Organisationen, die uns den Nachdruck bereits veröffentlichten Materials gestattet haben.

Die Evangelisch-Reformierte Kirchen im Kanton Bern, Schweiz, hat die Veröffentlichung dieses Buches finanziell unterstützt, und wir möchten uns für diese aufmerksame Geste herzlich bedanken.

Introducción

«Jesucristo, Vida del Mundo» es el tema de la Sexta Asamblea del Consejo Mundial de Iglesias que se reunirá en Vancouver (Canadá) del 24 de julio al 10 de agosto de 1983. Unos cuatro mil cristianos de todas partes del mundo se reunirán alrededor de ese tema. A la luz de la afirmación de que Jesuscristo es la vida del mundo, examinarán la labor y el testimonio del CMI durante los últimos siete años, y establecerán las directrices para su trabajo futuro.

El culto es una parte central del programa de la Asamblea. La labor de estudio y los debates se realizan dentro del marco del culto. Este libro se ha realizado con la convicción de que nuestro culto, tanto colectivo como individual, configurará e inspirará todo nuestro trabajo en la Asamblea.

En Vancouver, una gran parte del culto — las oraciones de alabanza y de acción de gracias, la confesión de los pecados, las intercesiones por toda la tierra habitada, la proclamación de la Palabra — se celebrará en una tienda de campaña destinada a este propósito. La tienda de campaña, signo del pueblo peregrino nos recuerda la imagen

de la Encarnación en el Evangelio de Juan: Dios en Jesucristo arma
una tienda de campaña con nosotros y para nosotros, así como para
toda su creación.

En la página xiii se encuentra una guía para el culto que se celebrará
diariamente por la mañana. Esta guía, preparada en un seminario
ecuménico internacional en marzo de 1982, está destinada a facilitar
a cristianos que hablan diferentes lenguas la celebración común del
culto en un espíritu de unidad.

La primera parte del libro contiene letanías, oraciones, pasajes bíblicos
y responsorios inspirados en los cuatro subtemas de la Asamblea.
La segunda parte contiene una colección de cánticos y alabanzas
cantadas también en relación con el tema de la Asamblea. Estos
cánticos están destinados a servir de complemento al himnario
ecuménico «Cantate Domino» publicado bajo los auspicios del CMI.

El Libro de Culto refleja la riqueza ecuménica de la Iglesia y presenta
una gran diversidad cultural y confesional. Contiene oraciones tradi-
cionales junto con oraciones contemporáneas y emplea un lenguaje
que se refiere a las mujeres y a los hombres. Sus autores esperan que
este libro contribuya a extender los horizontes litúrgicos y que las
personas que los utilicen compartan cánticos y formas cultuales de
cristianos que viven en otras culturas y tradiciones.

Aunque la finalidad inmediata de este libro es su uso en la Asamblea,
cabe esperar que también pueda enriquecer la vida cultual del pueblo
de Dios en el mundo entero durante los próximos años. Con esta
esperanza, el Comité de Culto para la Asamblea y el personal del
CMI que colabora con dicho Comité les saluda en nombre de
Jesucristo, Vida del Mundo.

* * *

Lamentamos que por razones de falta de espacio no nos sea posible
publicar todos los materiales litúrgicos en todas las lenguas de trabajo
del CMI.

Las respuestas están en letra bastardilla. Las mayúsculas pequeñas
(versalitas) indican que *todos* se unen a la oración o a la respuesta.

Deseamos expresar nuestro agradecimiento a todos los que han
aportado material para el libro de culto, así como a las personas y
organizaciones que nos han autorizado a utilizar textos ya publicados.

Las Iglesias Evangélicas Reformadas del cantón de Berna (Suiza) han
prestado ayuda financiera para la publicación de este libro, gesto por
el que les estamos muy agradecidos.

Order of daily worship

(Community singing)
Meditative music
Trinitarian invocation (by animators)   (Standing)
Doxology (Holy, Holy, Holy...)   "
Penitential psalm   (Sitting)
Confession   "
Entrance of the Word of God: (Standing)
   Procession of Gospel, light (Bread)
Bible reading
Acclamation
Meditation on the word
Intercessions — each followed by Kyrie Eleison   (Sitting)
Silent prayer
The Lord's Prayer   (Standing)
(The blessing of bread)
Benediction: "The grace..."
Singing

Ordre du culte journalier

(Chant...)
Musique de méditation
Invocation trinitaire (par les célébrants)   (Debout)
Doxologie (Saint, Saint, Saint...)   "
Psaume de pénitence   (Assis)
Confession   "
Entrée   (Debout)
   Procession avec l'évangile, lumière (Pain)
Lecture biblique
Acclamation
Méditation sur la Parole
Intercessions chacune suivie par Kyrie Eleison   (Assis)
Prière en silence
L'Oraison dominicale   (Debout)
(La Bénédiction du Pain)
La Bénédiction: «La Grâce...»
Chant

The peacock is a symbol of immortality, the vase a symbol of the water of life • *Le paon est symbole d'immortalité et le vase symbole de l'eau vive*

Ordnung des täglichen Gottesdienstes

(Gemeinsames Singen)	
Meditative Musik	
Trinitarische Eröffnung	(stehend)
Doxologie (Heilig, Heilig, Heilig…)	"
Busspsalm	(sitzend)
Bekenntnis	"
Prozession:	(stehend)
Hereinbringen von Bibel, Kerze (Brot)	
Bibellesung	
Akklamation	
Meditation über das Wort	
Fürbitten — aufgenommen mit Kyrie Eleison	(sitzend)
Stilles Gebet	
Vater unser	(stehend)
(Segnen des Brotes)	
Segen: «Die Gnade…»	
Singen	

Ordén de culto diario

(Comunidad cantando)	
Música de meditación	
Invocación a la Trinidad (por los animadores)	(de pie)
Doxologia (Santo, Santo, Santo…)	"
Salmo de penitencia	(sentados)
Confesión	"
Introducción de la Palabra de Dios:	(de pie)
Procesión del Evangelio, de la luz (el Pan)	
Lectura bíblica	
Aclamación	
Meditación sobre la Palabra	
Intercesiones… cada una seguida por el Kyrie Eleison	(sentados)
Oración en silencio	
La oración del Señor	(de pie)
(La bendición del Pan)	
Bendición: Que la gracia…	
Canto	

Der Pfau symbolisiert die Unsterblichkeit, der Kelch das Wasser des Lebens • *El pavo real es símbolo de inmortalidad y el jarrón simboliza el agua viva*

Life, a gift of God

La vie, don de Dieu

Leben, ein Geschenk Gottes

La vida, don de Dios

Life, by Marc Chagall (1964) • *La vie, de Marc Chagall* • Das Leben, von Marc Chagall • *La vida, de Marc Chagall*
© 1983, copyright by A.D.A.G.P., Paris & Cosmopress, Geneva

Life, a gift of God
La vie, don de Dieu
Leben, ein Geschenk Gottes
La vida, don de Dios

I. **Biblical affirmations** ● *Affirmations bibliques*
Biblische Leitsätze ● *Afirmaciones bíblicas*

▌1

a) Now the earth was a formless void; there was darkness over the deep, and God's spirit hovered over the water. God said, "Let there be light", and there was light (Genesis 1:2-3, JB).

b) "The spirit of God has made me and the breath of the Almighty gives me life" (Job 33:4, RSV).

c) "Listen! I, the Lord, am giving you a choice between the way that leads to life, and the way that leads to death" (Jeremiah 21:8, TEV).

d) The testimony is this: God has given us eternal life, and this life has its source in his Son (1 John 5:11, TEV).

II. **Scripture passages** ● *Extraits de l'Ecriture*
Bibelstellen ● *Pasajes de la Sagrada Escritura*

▌2

Psalms 8 and 104:	God's glory and human dignity
Psalm 139:	God's presence
Hosea 11:1-4, 8, 9:	God nurturing the people

Deuteronomy 30: 11-14, 19-20: The choice between life and death
John 1: 1-14:   The Word of Life
     3:16-21:   The new life
     6:36-40:   The Bread of Life
Acts 17:24-28:   Life in God

III. Responsive readings and litanies ● *Répons et litanies*
Responsorien und Litaneien ● *Responsorios y letanías*

3   *The longing for God*

Oh, come to the water all you who are thirsty;
Though you have no money, come!
Buy corn without money, and eat,
And, at no cost, wine and milk.

Psalm 42:2   I-to Loh, Taiwan

My soul— thirsts for God, for the liv - ing God.

Why spend money on what is not bread,
Your wages on what fails to satisfy?
Listen, listen to me, and you will have good things to eat
And rich food to enjoy.

My soul thirsts for God, for the living God!

Pay attention, come to me;
Listen, and your soul will live.
With you I will make an everlasting covenant.

My soul thirsts for God, for the living God!

Seek the Lord while he is still to be found,
Call to him while he is still near.

My soul thirsts for God, for the living God!

3   Verlangen nach Gott

Wohlan, alle, die ihr durstig seid, kommt her zum Wasser!
Und die ihr kein Geld habt, kommt her, kauft und esst!
Kommt her und kauft Wein und Milch,
ohne Geld und umsonst!

Meine Seele dürstet nach Gott, nach dem lebendigen Gott.

Warum zählt ihr Geld dar für das, was kein Brot ist,
und sauren Verdienst für das, was nicht satt macht?
Hört doch auf mich, so werdet ihr Gutes essen
und euch am Köstlichen laben.

Meine Seele dürstet nach Gott, nach dem lebendigen Gott.

Neigt eure Ohren her und kommt her zu mir!
Höret, so werdet ihr leben!
Ich will mit euch einen ewigen Bund schliessen.

Meine Seele dürstet nach Gott, nach dem lebendigen Gott.

Suchet den Herrn, solange er zu finden ist;
rufet ihn an, solange er nahe ist.

Meine Seele dürstet nach Gott, nach dem lebendigen Gott.

3   El anhelo de Dios

A todos los sedientos: venid a las aguas;
y los que no tienen dinero, venid, comprad y comed.
Venid, comprad sin dinero y sin precio,
vino y leche.

Mi alma tiene sed de Dios, del Dios vivo

¿Por qué gastáis el dinero en lo que no es pan,
y vuestro trabajo en lo que no sacia?
Oidme atentamente y comed del bien,
y se deleitará vuestra alma con grosura.

Mi alma tiene sed de Dios, del Dios vivo

Inclinad vuestro oído, y venid a mí;
oíd, y vivirá vuestra alma;
y haré con vosotros pacto eterno.

Mi alma tiene sed de Dios, del Dios vivo

Buscad al Señor mientras puede ser hallado,
llamadle en tanto que está cercano.

Mi alma tiene sed de Dios, del Dios vivo.

4   *Call us, yet again*

Creator God,
breathing your own life into our being,
you gave us the gift of life:
You placed us on this earth
     with its minerals and waters,
     flowers and fruits,
       living creatures of grace and beauty!
You gave us the care of the earth.

Today you call us:
"Where are you; what have you done?"

     (silence)

We hide in utter shame, for we are naked.
     We violate the earth and plunder it;
     We refuse to share the earth's resources;
     We seek to own what is not ours, but yours.

Forgive us, creator God, and reconcile us to your creation.

O God of Love
You gave us the gift of peoples —
     of cultures, races and colours,
     to love, to care for, to share our lives with.

Today you ask us:
"Where is your brother, your sister?"

     (silence)

We hide ourselves in shame and fear.
     Poverty, hunger, hatred and war rule the earth;
     The refugees, the oppressed and the voiceless
       cry out to you.

Forgive us, O God of love, and reconcile us to yourself and to one another.

Fowl my friend, by Aloi Pilioko • *Coq mon ami, d'Aloi Pilioko* • Mein Freund, der Hahn,
von Aloi Pilioko • *Mi amigo el gallo, de Aloi Pilioko*

TEACH US, O CREATOR GOD OF LOVE,
THAT THE EARTH AND ALL ITS FULLNESS IS YOURS,
THE WORLD AND THOSE WHO DWELL IN IT.
CALL US YET AGAIN TO SAFEGUARD THE GIFT OF LIFE.

4 *Appelle-nous, une fois encore*

Dieu créateur,
en nous insufflant ta propre vie,
tu nous as fait don de la vie:
Tu nous as placés sur cette terre
    avec ses minéraux et ses eaux,
    ses fleurs et ses fruits,
    et tous ses êtres vivants de grâce et de beauté!
Tu nous as confié le soin de la terre.

Aujourd'hui, tu nous appelles:
«Où êtes-vous? qu'avez-vous fait?»

    (silence)

Nous nous cachons de honte, car nous sommes nus.
    Nous violons la terre et la pillons;
    Nous refusons de partager les ressources de la terre;
    Nous cherchons à posséder ce qui est à toi.

Pardonne-nous, Dieu créateur, et réconcilie-nous avec ta création.

O Dieu d'amour
Tu nous as fait le don des peuples —
    des cultures, des races et des couleurs,
    pour aimer, pour soigner, pour partager nos vies.

Aujourd'hui tu nous demandes:
Où est ton frère, où est ta sœur?

    (silence)

Nous nous cachons de honte et de peur.
    La pauvreté, la faim, la haine et la guerre gouvernent la terre;
    Les réfugiés, les opprimés, ceux qui sont privés de voix crient vers
toi.

Pardonne-nous, Dieu d'amour, et réconcilie-nous avec toi et avec nos semblables.

ENSEIGNE-NOUS, O DIEU CRÉATEUR D'AMOUR,
QUE LA TERRE ET TOUTE SA PLÉNITUDE T'APPARTIENNENT,
LE MONDE ET CEUX QUI L'HABITENT.
APPELLE-NOUS UNE FOIS ENCORE POUR QUE NOUS GARDIONS LE DON
DE LA VIE.

4   *Llámanos, una vez más*

Dios creador;
al infundirnos tu propia vida
nos diste el don de vida:
Nos has puesto en esta tierra,
  con sus minerales y sus aguas,
  con sus flores y frutos,
  con sus criaturas vivas de gracia y belleza.
Nos encomendaste el cuidado de la tierra.

Hoy nos llamas:
«¿dónde estás? ¿qué has hecho?»

  (silencio)

Nos escondemos avergonzados, porque estamos desnudos.
  Hemos violado la tierra y la hemos saqueado;
  Nos negamos a compartir sus recursos;
  Intentamos poseer lo que no es nuestro, sino tuyo.

Perdónanos, Dios creador, y reconcílianos con tu creación.

Oh Dios de Amor
Nos has dado el don de los pueblos —
  de las culturas, razas y colores,
  para amar, para cuidar, para compartir nuestras vidas.

Nos preguntas hoy.
«¿dónde está tu hermano y tu hermana?»

  (silencio)

Nos escondemos con vergüenza y con miedo.
  La pobreza, el hambre, el odio y la guerra dominan la tierra;
  Los refugiados, los oprimidos y los enmudecidos claman a ti.

Perdónanos, oh Dios de amor, y reconcílianos contigo
y con nuestro prójimo.

ENSÉÑANOS, OH DIOS CREADOR, DIOS DE AMOR,
QUE LA TIERRA Y TODA SU PLENITUD ES TUYA,
EL MUNDO Y LOS QUE EN ÉL MORAN.
LLÁMANOS OTRA VEZ PARA QUE GUARDEMOS EL DON DE VIDA —

"God goes down deep", by Gaumana Gauwrrain • *Dieu
pénètre toute chose, de Gaumana Gauwrrain* • Gott dringt
tief in alle Dinge ein, von Gaumana Gauwrrain • *Dios
llega al fondo de todas las cosas, de Gaumana Gauwrrain*

5   *Donne-nous la vie*

Saint-Esprit, Créateur,
qui au commencement planais sur les eaux,
par ton souffle tous les êtres ont pris vie,
sans toi tout être vivant expire et retourne au néant,

Viens en nous, Saint-Esprit!

9

Saint-Esprit, Consolateur,
par toi nous sommes nés à la vie d'enfants de Dieu,
toi qui fais de nous des temples vivants de ta présence
et qui intercèdes au-dedans de nous par d'inexprimables supplications,

Viens en nous, Saint-Esprit!

Saint-Esprit, Seigneur qui donnes la vie,
tu es lumière et porteur de lumière,
tu es bonté et source de toute bonté,

Viens en nous, Saint-Esprit!

Saint-Esprit, Vivifiant,
toi qui animes et sanctifies tout le Corps de l'Eglise,
tu habites en chacun de ses membres
pour rendre un jour la vie à nos corps mortels,

Viens en nous, Saint-Esprit!

5   *Give us life*

Holy Spirit, Creator,
at the beginning you hovered over the waters;
you breathe life into all creatures;
without you every living creature dies and returns to nothingness,

Come into us, Holy Spirit.

Holy Spirit, Comforter,
by you we are born again as children of God;
you make us living temples of your presence,
you pray within us with prayers too deep for words,

Come into us, Holy Spirit.

Holy Spirit, Lord and Giver of Life,
you are light, you bring us light;
you are goodness and the source of all goodness,

Come into us, Holy Spirit.

Holy Spirit, Breath of life,
you sanctify and breathe life into the whole body of the Church;
you dwell in each one of its members,
and will one day give new life to our mortal bodies,

Come into us, Holy Spirit.

5   *Schenke uns Leben*

Heiliger Geist, Schöpfer,
am Anfang schwebstest du über den Wassern,
durch deinen Atem haben alle Geschöpfe Leben empfangen,
ohne dich erlischt alles Lebendige und fällt ins Nichts zurück.

Komm zu uns, Heiliger Geist!

Heiliger Geist, Tröster,
durch dich haben wir Leben als Kinder Gottes empfangen,
du machst uns zu lebendigen Tempeln deiner Gegenwart
und trittst für uns ein mit unaussprechlichen Bitten.

Komm zu uns, Heiliger Geist!

Heiliger Geist, Herr und Lebensspender
du bist Licht und Träger des Lichtes,
du bist Güte und Quelle aller Güte.

Komm zu uns, Heiliger Geist!

Heiliger Geist, Quelle des Lebens,
du hauchst dem ganzen Leib der Kirche Leben ein und heiligst ihn,
du wohnst in jedem seiner Glieder,
um unserem sterblichen Leib eines Tages ewiges Leben zu schenken.

Komm zu uns, Heiliger Geist!

IV. Prayers   •   *Prières*   •   Gebete   •   *Oraciones*

6   *Adoration*

O Supreme Lord of the Universe,
You fill and sustain everything around us;
With the touch of your hand you turned
chaos into order, darkness into light.
Unknown energies you hid in the heart of matter.
From you bursts forth the splendour of the sun,
and the mild radiance of the moon.
Stars and planets without number you set in ordered movement.
You are the source of the fire's heat and the wind's might,
of the water's coolness and the earth's stability.
Deep and wonderful are the mysteries of your creation.

We adore you, you are beyond all form!
You give form to everything, Lord of all creation.

Nativity, by S. E. Bottex • *Nativité, de S. E. Bottex* • Die Geburt Christi, von S. E. Bottex • *Natividad, de S. E. Bottex*

God of all salvation,
You formed us in your own image.
You created us male and female,
you willed our union and harmony.
You entrusted the earth to our care
and promised your blessing to all our descendants.
You gave us the spirit of discernment to know you,
the power of speech to celebrate your glory,
the strength of love to give ourselves in joy to you.
In this wondrous way, O God,
you called us to share
in your own being,
your own knowledge,
your own bliss.

In the Oneness of the Supreme Spirit,
through Christ who unites all things in his fullness
we and the whole creation give to you
honour and glory, thanks and praise,
worship and adoration,
now and in every age, for ever and ever. Amen.

6 *Adoration*

Seigneur suprême de l'Univers,
Tu combles et soutiens toutes choses autour de nous,
En les touchant de ta main, tu as changé
le chaos en bel ordre, la ténèbre en lumière.
Tu as caché au cœur de la matière des énergies inconnues.
De toi jaillit la splendeur du soleil,
et le doux rayonnement de la lune;
Tu as mis en mouvement ordonné étoiles et planètes sans nombre.
Tu es la source de l'ardeur du feu et de la force du vent,
de la fraîcheur des eaux et de la stabilité de la terre.
Profonds et merveilleux, les mystères de ta création.

Nous t'adorons, toi qui es au-delà de toute forme!
Tu donnes forme à toutes choses, Seigneur de toute création.

Dieu de toute libération,
tu nous as formés à ta propre image.
Tu nous as créés homme et femme,
tu as voulu notre union et harmonie.
Tu as confié la terre à nos soins
et tu as promis ta bénédiction à toute notre descendance.
Tu nous as donné l'esprit de discernement pour te connaître,

le pouvoir de la parole pour célébrer ta gloire,
la force de l'amour pour nous donner à toi dans la joie.
Sur ce chemin de merveilles, ô Dieu,
tu nous as appelés à partager
ton être-même,
ta propre connaissance,
ton intime joie.

Dans l'unité de l'Esprit-Saint,
par le Christ qui unit tout en sa plénitude
nous et la création tout entière, nous te rendons
honneur et gloire, louange et action de grâce,
notre culte d'adoration,
maintenant et toujours, pour les siècles des siècles. Amen.

6   Anbetung

Höchster Herr des Alls,
Du füllst und erhältst alles um uns herum,
Du hast durch das Berühren mit Deiner Hand
Chaos in Ordnung, Dunkelheit in Licht verwandelt.
Unbekannte Energien hast Du im Innern der Materie verborgen.
Aus Dir bricht der Glanz der Sonne
und das milde Strahlen des Mondes.
Unzählige Sterne und Planeten hast Du in geordnete Bahnen gelenkt.
Du bist die Quelle der Glut des Feuers und der Macht des Windes,
der Frische des Wassers und der Beständigkeit der Erde.
Unergründlich und wundervoll sind die Geheimnisse Deiner
    Schöpfung.

Wir beten Dich an, der Du über allem stehst!
Du gibst jedem Ding Gestalt, Herr der ganzen Schöpfung.

Gott allen Heils,
Du hast uns nach Deinem eigenen Bild gestaltet,
Du hast uns als Mann und Frau geschaffen,
Du hast unsere Übereinstimmung und Harmonie gewollt.
Du hast uns die Pflege der Erde anvertraut
und all unseren Nachfahren Deinen Segen verheissen.
Du hast uns den Geist der Wahrnehmung verliehen, Dich zu
    erkennen,
die Macht der Sprache, Deinen Ruhm zu verkünden,
die Kraft der Liebe, uns Dir in Freude hinzugeben.
Auf diesem wunderbaren Weg, o Gott,
hast Du uns berufen, teilzunehmen
an Deinem eigenen Sein,

14

an Deinem eigenen Wissen,
an Deiner eigenen Freude.

In dem Einssein mit dem Höchsten Geist
durch Christus, der alle Dinge in seiner Fülle vereint,
geben wir und die ganze Schöpfung Dir
Ehre und Ruhm, Dank und Lob,
Verehrung und Anbetung,
jetzt und immerdar, von Ewigkeit zu Ewigkeit. Amen.

7   *The joy of creation*

We give you thanks, most gracious God,
for the beauty of earth and sea;
for the richness of mountains, plains, and rivers;
for the songs of birds and the loveliness of flowers.
We praise you for these good gifts,
and pray that we may safeguard them for our posterity.
Grant that we may grow in our grateful enjoyment
of your abundant creation;
to the honour and glory of your Name, now and for ever. Amen.

7   *Die Freude der Schöpfung*

Wir sagen dir Dank, gnädiger Gott,
für die Schönheit der Erde und des Meeres;
für den Reichtum der Berge, Ebenen und Flüsse;
für das Singen der Vögel und die Lieblichkeit der Blumen.
Für alle diese guten Gaben loben wir dich und bitten,
dass wir sie schützen mögen für die, die nach uns kommen.
Hilf uns, dass wir wachsen in Dankbarkeit für deine reiche Schöpfung
und in unserer Freude an ihr,
zur Ehre und zum Preis deines Namens,
jetzt und immerdar.

7   *La alegría de la Creación*

Te damos gracia, Dios misericordioso,
por la belleza de la tierra y del mar;
por la riqueza de las montañas, llanuras y ríos;
por el canto de los pájaros y la hermosura de las flores.
Te alabamos por todos esos dones,

y rogamos a fin de que podamos conservarlos para la posteridad.
Concédenos que podamos seguir disfrutando
con gratitud de la abundancia de la creación
para honor y gloria de tu Nombre, ahora y siempre. Amén.

8   *The glory of creation*

Lord of lords, Creator of all things, God of all things, God over all
  gods, God of sun and rain, you created the earth with a thought
  and us with your breath.
Lord, we brought in the harvest. The rain watered the earth, the
  sun drew cassava and corn out of the clay. Your mercy showered
  blessing after blessing over our country. Creeks grew into rivers;
  swamps became lakes. Healthy fat cows graze on the green sea
  of the savanna. The rain smoothed out the clay walls; the
  mosquitoes perished in the high waters.
Lord, the yam is fat like meat, the cassava melts on the tongue,
  oranges burst in their peels, dazzling and bright.
Lord, nature gives thanks, your creatures give thanks. Your praise
  rises in us like the great river.
Lord of lords, Creator, Provider, we thank you in the name of Jesus
  Christ. Amen.

8   *La gloire de la création*

Seigneur des seigneurs, créateur de toutes choses,
  Dieu de toutes choses, Dieu au-dessus de tous
  les dieux, Dieu du soleil et de la pluie, tu as créé
  la terre d'une pensée, et ton souffle nous a donné vie.
Seigneur, nous avons rentré la moisson. La pluie a arrosé
  la terre, le soleil a tiré de l'argile le manioc et le blé. Ta
  miséricorde a déversé sur notre pays bienfaits sur bienfaits.
  Les ruisseaux se sont changés en rivières, et les étangs en lacs.
  Ce sont des vaches grasses qui paissent dans le vert océan de
  la savane. Les pluies ont poli les murs d'argile; les grandes
  eaux ont emporté les moustiques.
Seigneur, l'igname est grasse comme de la viande, le manioc fond
  dans la bouche, les oranges sont éclatantes et gonflées de jus.
Seigneur, la nature rend grâce, tes créatures rendent grâce. Ta louange
  monte en nous comme la grande rivière.
Seigneur des seigneurs, créateur et providence, nous te remercions
  au nom de Jésus-Christ. Amen.

Pomegranate: symbol of God's goodness • *Grenade: symbole de la bonté de Dieu* • Der
Granatapfel, Symbol der Güte Gottes • *La granada, símbolo de la bondad de Dios*

16

Señor Dios, Creador de todas las cosas, Dios de todas las cosas,
    Dios sobre todos los dioses, Dios del sol y de la lluvia; creaste
    la tierra con un pensamiento y a nosotros con tu aliento.
Señor, hemos recogido la cosecha. La lluvia regó la tierra, el sol
    extrajo del barro mandioca y maíz. Tu misericordia derramó
    bendiciones sin fin sobre nuestro país. Los riachuelos se hicieron
    ríos; los pantanos se convirtieron en lagos. Vacas gordas y
    sanas pastan en la verde sabana. La lluvia ha pulido los muros
    de barro; los mosquitos perecieron en las riadas.
Señor, la batata es tan nutritiva como la carne, la mandioca se
    deshace en la boca, las naranjas están llenas de jugo y
    deslumbrantes.
Señor, la naturaleza te da las gracias, tus criaturas te dan las gracias.
    Tu alabanza crece en nosotros como el río.
Señor Dios, Creador, Dispensador, te damos gracias en nombre de
    Jesucristo. Amén.

Life confronting and overcoming death
La vie victorieuse de la mort

Leben und Tod:
Konfrontation und Überwindung
La vida hace frente y vence a la muerte

Entombment, by Rosemary Namuli • *Mise au tombeau, de Rosemary Namuli* • Begräbnis, von Rosemary Namuli • *Entierro, de Rosemary Namuli*

Life confronting and overcoming death
La vie victorieuse de la mort
Leben und Tod:
Konfrontation und Überwindung
La vida hace frente y vence a la muerte

I. Biblical affirmations ● ***Affirmations bibliques***
Biblische Leitsätze ● *Afirmaciones bíblicas*

9

a) I know that the Lord maintains the cause of the afflicted, and executes justice for the needy (Psalm 140:12, RSV).

b) He makes wars to cease to the end of the earth;
he breaks the bow, and shatters the spear,
he burns the chariots with fire (Psalm 46:9, RSV).

c) "Why are you looking among the dead for one who is alive?
He is not here; he has been raised" (Luke 24:5-6, TEV).

d) "Whoever believes in me will live even though he/she dies; and whoever lives and believes in me will never die"
(John 11:25-26, TEV).

The pelican symbolizes Christ's sacrifice on the cross. According to legend, it pierces its breast to feed its offspring with its own blood ● *Le pélican symbolise le sacrifice du Christ sur la croix. D'après la légende, il se perce le cœur pour nourrir ses enfants de son propre sang* ● Der Pelikan symbolisiert Christi Opfer am Kreuz. Einer Legende zufolge durchbohrt er seine Brust, um seine Jungen mit seinem eigenen Blut zu nähren ● *El pelícano simboliza el sacrificio de Cristo en la cruz. Según la leyenda, se perfora el pecho con el pico para alimentar a sus crías con su propia sangre.*

e) "For whoever wants to save his / her own life will lose it; but whoever loses his/her life for me and the gospel will save it" (Mark 8:35, TEV).

II. Scripture passages ● *Extraits de l'Ecriture*
   Bibelstellen ● *Pasajes de la Sagrada Escritura*

■ 10

Isaiah 40:1-8:   The voice in the wilderness
Ezekiel 37:1-14:   The vision of the valley of dry bones
Mark 8:31-9:1:   The way of the cross
Romans 6:7-11:   Dead to sin, but alive in Christ
1 Corinthians 15:12-20: The ground of hope
Hebrews 13:12-16:   Outside the city walls
1 John 3:11-18:   Love in action

III. Responsive readings and litanies ● *Répons et litanies*
   Responsorien und Litaneien ● *Responsorios y letanías*

■ 11   *Creation in travail*

The sufferings of this present time are not worth comparing with the glory that is to be revealed.

I saw a new heaven and a new earth, for the former things had passed away.

The creation waits with eager longing for the revealing of the children of God.

I saw a new heaven and a new earth, for the former things had passed away.

The creation was subjected to futility, not of its own will but by the will of him who subjected it in hope.

I saw a new heaven and a new earth, for the former things had passed away.

The creation itself will be set free from its bondage to decay and obtain the glorious liberty of the children of God.

I saw a new heaven and a new earth, for the former things had passed away.

22

The whole creation has been groaning in travail together until now; and not only the creation, but we ourselves, who have the first fruit of the Spirit, groan inwardly as we wait for adoption as sons and daughters, the redemption of our bodies.

I saw a new heaven and a new earth, for the former things had passed away.

11   *La création dans les douleurs de l'enfantement*

Les souffrances du temps présent sont sans proportion avec la gloire qui doit être révélée.

Je vis un ciel nouveau et une terre nouvelle, car les premiers ont disparu.

La création attend avec impatience la révélation des enfants de Dieu.

Je vis un ciel nouveau et une terre nouvelle, car les premiers ont disparu.

Livrée au pouvoir du néant — non de son propre gré, mais par l'autorité de celui qui l'y a livrée — la création garde l'espérance.

Je vis un ciel nouveau et une terre nouvelle, car les premiers ont disparu.

Elle aussi sera libérée de l'esclavage de la corruption, pour avoir part à la liberté et à la gloire des enfants de Dieu.

Je vis un ciel nouveau et une terre nouvelle, car les premiers ont disparu.

La création tout entière gémit maintenant encore dans les douleurs de l'enfantement. Elle n'est pas la seule, nous aussi, qui possédons les prémices de l'Esprit, nous gémissons intérieurement, attendant l'adoption, la délivrance pour notre corps.

Je vis un ciel nouveau et une terre nouvelle, car les premiers ont disparu.

11   *Schöpfung in Geburtswehen*

Die Leiden dieser Zeit sind der Herrlichkeit nicht wert, die an uns offenbart werden soll.

Ich sah einen neuen Himmel und eine neue Erde; denn das Erste war vergangen.

Die Kreatur harrt ängstlich auf die Offenbarung der Kinder Gottes.

Ich sah einen neuen Himmel und eine neue Erde; denn das Erste war vergangen.

Die Kreatur ist der Vergänglichkeit unterworfen, ohne ihren Willen, sondern um dessen willen, der sie unterworfen hat — auf Hoffnung hin.

Ich sah einen neuen Himmel und eine neue Erde; denn das Erste war vergangen.

Die Kreatur wird frei werden von der Knechtschaft des vergänglichen Wesens zu der herrlichen Freiheit der Kinder Gottes.

Ich sah einen neuen Himmel und eine neue Erde; denn das Erste war vergangen.

Alle Kreatur sehnt sich mit uns und ängstigt sich noch immerdar. Nicht aber allein sie, sondern auch wir selbst, die wir haben des Geistes Erstlingsgabe, sehnen uns auch bei uns selbst nach der Kindschaft und warten auf unseres Leibes Erlösung.

Ich sah einen neuen Himmel und eine neue Erde; denn das Erste war vergangen.

12 Ein Akt der Busse

O Herr, unsere Herzen sind schwer
vom Leid der Zeiten
von den Kreuzzügen und Vernichtungsaktionen der Jahrtausende.
Das Blut der Opfer ist noch warm.
Noch füllen die Schreie des Zorns die Nacht.

Wir erheben unsere Hände zu dir.

Wir dürsten nach dir in dürrem Land.

O Herr, du liebst uns wie ein Vater,
du sorgst für uns wie eine Mutter.
Wie ein Bruder hast du unser Leben geteilt.
Wir bekennen vor dir, dass wir nicht fähig sind, als deine Kinder zu
    leben,
als Brüder und Schwestern verbunden durch dasselbe Band der Liebe.

Wir erheben unsere Hände zu dir.

Wir dürsten nach dir in dürrem Land.

Das Geschenk des Lebens haben wir verschleudert.
Das gute Leben einiger
gründet auf dem Leiden der Vielen,
das Vergnügen der Wenigen
auf der Not von Millionen.

Wir erheben unsere Hände zu dir.

Wir dürsten nach dir in dürrem Land.

"We're OK. We're waiting for news from you", by Ismail Schammut • *«Nous allons bien. Nous attendons de vos nouvelles», d'Ismail Schammut* • «Uns geht's gut. Wir warten auf Nachricht von euch», von Ismail Schammut • *«Estamos bien. Esperando que nos lleguen tus noticias», de Ismail Schammut*

Den Tod beten wir an, in unserer Sucht immer mehr zu besitzen;
den Tod beten wir an,
in unserer atemlosen Suche nach unserer eigenen
Sicherheit, unserem eigenen Überleben, unserem eigenen Frieden.
Als ob das Leben teilbar wäre,
als ob die Liebe teilbar wäre,
als ob Christus nicht für alle gestorben ist.

Wir erheben unsere Hände zu dir.

Wir dürsten nach dir in dürrem Land.

O Herr, vergib uns unsere Jagd nach dem Leben, die das Leben
    verneint.
Und hilf uns, neu zu verstehen, was es heisst,
deine Kinder zu sein.

Wir erheben unsere Hände zu dir.

Wir dürsten nach dir in dürrem Land.

12   An act of penitence

O Lord, our hearts are heavy
with the sufferings of the ages,
with the crusades and the holocausts
of a thousand thousand years.
The blood of the victims is still warm,
The cries of anguish still fill the night.

To you we lift our outspread hands.

We thirst for you in a thirsty land.

O Lord, who loves us as a father,
who cares for us as a mother,
who came to share our life as a brother,
we confess before you our failure to live as your children,
brothers and sisters bound together in love.

To you we lift our outspread hands.

We thirst for you in a thirsty land.

We have squandered the gift of life.
The good life of some
is built on the pain of many;
the pleasure of a few
on the agony of millions.

To you we lift our outspread hands.

We thirst for you in a thirsty land.

We worship death in our quest to possess ever more things;
we worship death in our hankering after
our own security, our own survival, our own peace,
as if life were divisible
as if love were divisible
as if Christ had not died for all of us.

To you we lift our outspread hands.

We thirst for you in a thirsty land.

O Lord, forgive our life-denying pursuit of life,
and teach us anew what it means to be your children.

To you we lift our outspread hands.

We thirst for you in a thirsty land.

12 *Acto de Penitencia*

Oh Señor, nuestros corazones llevan el peso
de los sufrimientos de todos los tiempos,
de las cruzadas y los holocaustos
de miles y miles de años.
La sangre de las víctimas está aún caliente.
Los gritos de congoja todavía resuenan en la noche.

Hacia ti extendemos nuestras manos.

Tenemos sed de tí en una tierra sedienta.

Oh Señor, que nos amas como un padre,
que nos cuidas como una madre,
que viniste a compartir nuestra vida como un hermano,
te confesamos nuestro fracaso en vivir como tus hijos,
como hermanos y hermanas unidos por el amor.

Hacia ti extendemos nuestras manos.

Tenemos sed de tí en una tierra sedienta.

Hemos malgastado el don de vida.
La buena vida de algunos
se basa en el dolor de muchos;
el placer de unos pocos
en la agonía de millones.

Hacia ti extendemos nuestras manos.

Tenemos sed de tí en una tierra sedienta.

Rendimos culto a la muerte al querer poseer más y más cosas;
rendimos culto a la muerte cuando anhelamos
nuestra propia seguridad, nuestra propia supervivencia, nuestra
    propia paz;
como si la vida fuera divisible
como si el amor fuera divisible
como si Cristo no hubiera muerto por todos nosotros.

Hacia ti extendemos nuestras manos

Tenemos sed de tí en una tierra sedienta.

Oh Señor, perdónanos nuestra manera de vivir, que niega la vida,
y enséñanos de nuevo lo que significa ser hijos tuyos.

Hacia ti extendemos nuestras manos.

Tenenos sed de tí en una tierra sedienta.

13   *Empower us, O Lord!*

... When Jesus came ashore, he saw a great crowd;
and his heart went out to them...
As the day wore on, his disciples came up to him and said,
"This is a lonely place and it is getting very late;
send the people off to the farms and villages round about,
to buy themselves something to eat."
"Give them something to eat yourselves,"
he answered...

    (silence)

Lord, we remember the millions in our world
who must go hungry today,
all those who do not have even the basic necessities of life,
and for whom life itself has become a burden ...

Out of the depths we cry to you, Lord,
*Hear our cry and listen to our prayer.**

... Jesus was left alone with the woman, who remained
standing there.
He looked up and said, "Woman, where are they? Has no one
condemned you?"
"No one, Sir," she replied.
"Neither do I condemn you," said Jesus, "go away, and
don't sin anymore."

    (silence)

---

* Alternative sung response on facing page.

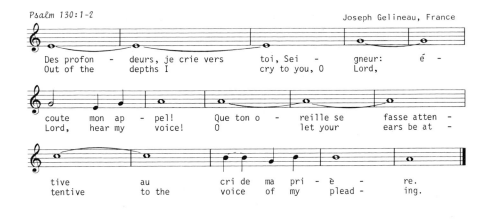

Psalm 130:1-2   Joseph Gelineau, France

Des profon - deurs, je crie vers toi, Sei - gneur: é -
Out of the depths I cry to you, 0 Lord,

coute mon ap - pel! Que ton o - reille se fasse atten -
Lord, hear my voice! 0 let your ears be at -

tive au cri de ma pri - è - re.
tentive to the voice of my plead - ing.

Lord we remember all those who, because of their caste or class,
colour or sex, are exploited and marginalized —
the forces of oppression that trample on people and
the unjust systems which break the spirit of people,
and rob them of their rights and dignity.

Out of the depths we cry to you, Lord,
Hear our cry and listen to our prayer.

... Now a priest happened to be travelling down the same road,
but when he saw the man, he passed by on the other side ...

    (silence)

Lord, we bring before you the churches and
the Christian people around the world.
Often we have remained silent, passing by on the other side;
Often we have been indifferent;
Often we have been part of the forces that destroy life.

Out of the depths we cry to you, Lord,
Hear our cry and listen to our prayer.

Pilate now took Jesus and had him flogged;
and the soldiers plaited a crown of thorns and placed it
on his head, and robed him in purple cloak...
He asked Jesus, "Where have you come from?"
But Jesus gave him no answer.
"Do you refuse to speak to me?" said Pilate. "Surely you know
that I have authority to release you, and I have authority
to crucify you"...

    (silence)

29

Lord, we call to mind all authority that treats people as nobodies —
Military regimes and dictatorships,
lonely prisons and unjust laws;
the war industry and political greed.

Out of the depths we cry to you, Lord,
Hear our cry and listen to our prayer.

Jesus stood up to read.
He opened the scroll and found the passage which says,
"The Spirit of the Lord is upon me;
he has sent me to announce good news to the poor,
to proclaim release for prisoners
and recovery of sight for the blind;
to let the broken victims go free,
to proclaim the year of the Lord's favour."

(silence)

Lord, we affirm with hope your presence in the world.
You see the wounded and the broken, and say—
"These are my brothers and sisters."

Lord inspire us with your love,
Challenge us with your truth,
Empower us with your strength
To live for life in the midst of death.

13 *Donne-nous ta force, Seigneur*

... En débarquant, Jésus vit une grande foule.
Il fut pris de pitié pour eux...
Comme il était déjà tard, ses disciples s'approchèrent de lui pour
lui dire: «L'endroit est désert et il est déjà tard. Renvoie-les;
qu'ils aillent dans les hameaux et les villages des environs s'acheter
de quoi manger». Mais il leur répondit: «Donnez-leur vous-mêmes à
manger».

(silence)

Seigneur, nous nous souvenons des millions d'êtres humains
qui, dans le monde, auront faim aujourd'hui,
de tous ceux qui n'ont même pas le strict nécessaire pour vivre
et à qui la vie pèse...

Des profondeurs nous crions vers toi, Seigneur,
*Entends notre cri, écoute notre prière.**

---

* Le répons peut être chanté. Voir p. 29.

... Jésus resta seul. Comme la femme était toujours là, au milieu du cercle, Jésus se redressa et lui dit: «Femme, où sont-ils donc? Personne ne t'a condamnée?»
Elle répondit: «Personne, Seigneur»
et Jésus lui dit: «Moi non plus, je ne te condamne pas: va, et désormais ne pèche plus.»

(silence)

Seigneur, nous nous souvenons de tous ceux qui sont exploités et marginalisés
à cause de leur caste ou de leur classe, de leur couleur ou de leur sexe.
Des forces de l'oppression écrasent les êtres humains, et des systèmes injustes les abattent, et les dépouillent de leurs droits et de leur dignité.

Des profondeurs nous crions vers toi, Seigneur,
Entends notre cri, écoute notre prière.

... Il se trouva qu'un prêtre descendait par ce chemin; il vit l'homme et passa à bonne distance...

(silence)

Seigneur, nous te présentons les Eglises
et les chrétiens du monde entier
Nous avons souvent gardé le silence, passant à bonne distance;
Nous avons souvent été indifférents;
Nous avons souvent fait partie des forces qui tuent.

Des profondeurs, nous crions vers toi, Seigneur,
Entends notre cri, écoute notre prière.

Alors Pilate emmena Jésus et le fit fouetter.
Les soldats, qui avaient tressé une couronne avec des épines, la lui mirent sur la tête et il jetèrent sur lui un manteau de pourpre...
Il dit à Jésus: «D'où est-tu, toi?» Mais Jésus ne lui fit aucune réponse.
Pilate lui dit alors: «C'est à moi que tu refuses de parler! Ne sais-tu pas que j'ai le pouvoir de te relâcher comme j'ai le pouvoir de te faire crucifier?»...

(silence)

Seigneur, nous évoquons toutes les autorités qui traitent les gens comme des quantités négligeables, les dictatures et les régimes militaires,
la solitude des prisons et les lois, l'industrie de la guerre et l'avidité politique.

Des profondeurs, nous crions vers toi, Seigneur,
Entends notre cri, écoute notre prière.

Jésus se leva pour faire la lecture.

En déroulant le livre, il trouva le passage où il était écrit:
«L'Esprit du Seigneur est sur moi;
il m'a envoyé annoncer la bonne nouvelle aux pauvres,
proclamer aux captifs la libération
et aux aveugles le retour à la vue,
renvoyer les opprimés en liberté,
proclamer une année d'accueil par le Seigneur»

(silence)

Seigneur, nous affirmons avec espérance ta présence dans le monde.
Tu vois des êtres blessés et déchirés, et tu dis:
«Voici mes frères et mes sœurs.»

Seigneur, inspire-nous de ton amour,
Interpelle-nous par ta vérité,
Donne-nous la force
De vivre pour la vie au milieu de la mort.

13 *¡Danos poder, Oh Señor!*

... Al bajar Jesús de la barca, vió la multitud,
y sintió compasión de ellos...
Por la tarde, sus discípulos se le acercaron y le dijeron:
–Ya es tarde, y éste es un lugar solitario. Despide a la gente
para que vayan por los campos y las aldeas y se compren algo de comer.
Pero Jesús les contestó: — Denles ustedes de comer...

(silencio)

Señor, hoy nos acordamos de los millones de hambrientos
en nuestro mundo,
de todos aquellos que ni siquiera tienen lo necesario para vivir,
Y para quienes la vida misma es una carga...

De lo profundo clamamos a ti, Señor,
escucha nuestro clamor y atiende nuestra oración.

... Cuando Jesús se encontró solo con la mujer, que se había quedado
allí, se enderezó y le preguntó: — Mujer, ¿dónde están? ¿Ninguno te ha
condenado?. Ella le contestó: Ninguno Señor.
Jesús le dijo: Tampoco yo te condeno; ahora vete y no vuelvas a pecar.

(silencio)

Señor, nos acordamos de todos los que son explotados y marginados
por pertenecer a cierta casta o clase, color o sexo. De las fuerzas

32

de la opresión que atropellan a las gentes y de los sistemas injustos
que quiebran el espíritu del pueblo, y le quitan su derecho y su dignidad.

De lo profundo clamamos a ti, Señor,
escucha nuestro clamor y atiende nuestra súplica.

… Por casualidad, un sacerdote pasaba por el mismo camino; pero al verle,
dió un rodeo y siguió adelante…

(silencio)

Señor, presentamos ante ti a las iglesias y al pueblo cristiano
de todo el mundo. Con frecuencia hemos permanecido en silencio,
evitando la realidad; con frecuencia hemos sido indiferentes, con
frecuencia hemos formado parte de las fuerzas que destruyen la vida.

De lo profundo clamamos a ti, Señor,
escucha nuestro clamor y atiende nuestra súplica.

Pilato tomó entonces a Jesús y mandó azotarlo. Los soldados trenzaron
una corona de espinas, la pusieron en la cabeza de Jesús y lo vistieron
con una capa de color rojo oscuro…
Y le preguntó a Jesús: ¿De dónde eres tú? Pero Jesús no le contestó nada.
Pilato le dijo: ¿Es que no me vas a contestar?. ¿No sabes que tengo autoridad
para crucificarte, lo mismo que para ponerte en libertad?

(silencio)

Señor, nos acordamos de todas las autoridades que tratan a la gente como si
no fueran personas, de los regímenes militares y dictatoriales,
de las prisiones solitarias y de las leyes injustas; de la industria bélica y
la voracidad política.

De lo profundo clamamos a ti, Señor
escucha nuestro clamor y atiende nuestra súplica.

Jesús se puso de pie, le dieron a leer el libro del profeta Isaías y
al abrirlo encontró el lugar donde estaba escrito:
«El Espíritu del Señor está sobre mí,
porque me ha consagrado
para llevar la buena noticia a los pobres;
me ha enviado a anunciar
libertad a los presos
y dar vista a los ciegos;
a poner en libertad a los oprimidos;
a anunciar el año favorable del Señor».

(silencio)

Señor, afirmamos con esperanza tu presencia en el mundo.
Tu miras a los heridos y a los quebrantados y dices: «Estos
son mi hermanos y mis hermanas».

Señor, inspíranos con tu amor
desafíanos con tu verdad,
Danos poder con tu fuerza
para vivir por la vida en medio de la muerte.

IV. Prayers • *Prières* • Gebete • *Oraciones*

14   *Celebration of life*

In the midst of hunger and war
  we celebrate the promise of plenty and peace.
In the midst of oppression and tyranny
  we celebrate the promise of service and freedom.
In the midst of doubt and despair
  we celebrate the promise of faith and hope,
In the midst of fear and betrayal
  we celebrate the promise of joy and loyalty.
In the midst of hatred and death
  we celebrate the promise of love and life.
In the midst of sin and decay
  we celebrate the promise of salvation and renewal.
In the midst of death on every side
  we celebrate the promise of the living Christ.

14   *Feier des Lebens*

Mitten in Hunger und Krieg
  feiern wir, was verheißen ist: Fülle und Frieden.
Mitten in Drangsal und Tyrannei
  feiern wir, was verheißen ist: Hilfe und Freiheit.
Mitten in Zweifel und Verzweiflung
  feiern wir, was verheißen ist: Glauben und Hoffnung.
Mitten in Furcht und Verrat
  feiern wir, was verheißen ist: Freude und Treue.

The butterfly is a symbol of the resurrection of Christ • *Le papillon est le symbole de la résurrection du Christ* • Der Schmetterling ist ein Symbol der Auferstehung Christi • *La mariposa es el símbolo de la resurrección de Cristo*

Mitten in Haß und Tod
feiern wir, was verheißen ist: Liebe und Leben.
Mitten in Sünde und Hinfälligkeit
feiern wir, was verheißen ist: Rettung und Neubeginn.
Mitten im Tod, der uns von allen Seiten umgibt,
feiern wir, was verheißen ist
durch den lebendigen Christus.

14   *Celebración de la vida*

En medio del hambre y la guerra
celebramos la promesa de abundancia y paz.
En medio de la opresión y la tiranía
celebramos la promesa de servicio y libertad.
En medio de la duda y la desesperación
celebramos la promesa de fe y esperanza,
En medio del miedo y la traición
celebramos la promesa de alegría y lealtad.
En medio del odio y la muerte
celebramos la promesa de amor y vida.
En medio del pecado y la ruina.
celebramos la promesa de salvación y renovación.
En medio de la muerte que nos rodea
celebramos la promesa del Cristo vivo.

15   *For peace*

We praise you, Holy Spirit, our Advocate and Comforter.
Help us to affirm life
in the midst of death,
supporting us as we confront the power of destruction,
urging us to hammer swords into ploughs
and spears into pruning knives;
so that wolves and sheep
live together in peace,
life is celebrated,
creation is restored
as the sphere of the living.
Holy Spirit, we praise you;
help us to affirm life
in the midst of death.

15   *Pour la paix*

Nous te louons, Saint-Esprit, notre défenseur et consolateur.
  Aide nous à proclamer la vie
    dans le domaine de la mort,
  soutiens nous lorsque nous affrontons les puissances de destruction,
  contrains nous à forger des charrues avec les épées,
    des serpes avec les lances,
  afin que loups et brebis
    puissent vivre ensemble dans la paix,
  que la vie soit célébrée,
    la création restaurée
    comme le domaine du vivant.
Saint-Esprit, nous te louons,
  car tu nous aides à proclamer la vie
    dans le domaine de la mort.

15   *Für Frieden*

Wir preisen dich, Heiliger Geist, unser Anwalt und Tröster.
  Hilf uns, zum Leben Ja zu sagen
    inmitten des Todes,
  unterstütze uns, der Macht des Todes entgegenzutreten,
  dränge uns dazu, Schwerter in Pflugscharen zu schmieden
    und Speerspitzen in Winzermesser;
  so daß Wölfe und Schafe
    in Frieden beisammen leben,
  daß das Leben gefeiert
    und die Schöpfung wiederhergestellt wird
    als ein Reich für alle, die leben.
Heiliger Geist, wir preisen dich,
  weil du uns hilfst, zum Leben Ja zu sagen
    inmitten des Todes.

16   *Prayer of intercession*

Lord,
God of justice and peace
who stands with those who are poor,
who asks us to be the voice of the voiceless,
we call upon you
for those who have suffered the injustices of war and greed.

From the depths of our being we cry to you, Lord.

Hear our cry, and listen to our prayers.

36

For those of Hiroshima and Nagasaki,
    Bikini and Enitwetok,
    Kwajalein and Mururoa,
    Fangataufa and Christmas Island,
    Johnston Island and Monte Bello,
    Emu and Maralinga:
Those Pacific people whose precious land and sea have been ravaged by
nuclear explosions.

From the depths of our being we cry to you, Lord.

Hear our cry, and listen to our prayers.

For those who are suffering this day from disease, genetic malformation
and the loss of those they love, as a result of nuclear radiation.
May their spirits not be broken by their bodies' pain.

From the depths of our being we cry to you, Lord.

Hear our cry, and listen to our prayers.

For those whose land and sea are today being put at risk through
radio-active pollution, from the dumping of nuclear wastes, and
the passage of nuclear ships.
May their livelihood and health be preserved and may they live in
peace and hope.

From the depths of our being we cry to you, Lord.

Hear our cry, and listen to our prayers.

We pray that your promise of justice may become real
to those for whom we pray.
May they be released to live in freedom and love.

From the depths of our being we cry to you, Lord.

Hear our cry and listen to our prayers,
for you are gracious, and there is in you
that which is to be feared, that which forgives,
that which strengthens, and that which comforts. Amen.

16 *Prière d'intercession*

Seigneur,
Dieu de justice et de paix,
toi qui es aux côtés des pauvres et
    nous demandes d'être la voix des sans-voix,
nous te prions
pour ceux qui ont connu les injustices de la guerre et de la cupidité.

Des profondeurs de notre être, nous crions vers toi, Seigneur.

Entends notre cri, écoute nos prières.

Pour les habitants de Hiroshima et de Nagasaki,
    de Bikini et d'Eniwetok,
    de Kwajalein et de Mururoa.
    de Fangataufa et de l'île Christmas,
    de l'île Johnston et de Monte Bello,
    d'Emu et de Maralinga.
Pour ces peuples du Pacifique qui ont vu leur précieuse terre et
leur océan ravagés par des explosions nucléaires.

Des profondeurs de notre être, nous crions vers toi, Seigneur.

Entends notre cri, écoute nos prières.

Pour ceux qui, à cause des radiations atomiques, souffrent aujourd'hui
de maladie, de malformation génétique et de la perte d'êtres chers.
Puisse la souffrance de leurs corps laisser intacts leurs esprits.

Des profondeurs de notre être, nous crions vers toi, Seigneur.

Entends notre cri, écoute nos prières.

Pour ceux dont les terres et les mers sont aujourd'hui menacées
par la pollution radioactive en raison du dépôt de déchets nucléaires
et du passage de vaisseaux nucléaires.
Que soient préservés leurs moyens d'existence et leur santé, et qu'ils
puissent vivre dans la paix et l'espérance.

Des profondeurs de notre être, nous crions vers toi, Seigneur.

Entends notre cri, écoute nos prières.

Que ta promesse de justice devienne réalité pour tous, nous t'en prions.
Puissent-ils être tous libérés, pour vivre dans l'amour et la liberté.

Des profondeurs de notre être, nous crions vers toi, Seigneur.

Entends nos cris, écoute nos prières,
car tu es miséricordieux, et tu es à la fois
celui qu'il faut craindre et celui qui pardonne,
celui qui fortifie et celui qui console. Amen.

16   *Oración de intercesión*

Señor,
Dios de justicia y de paz
que estás al lado de los pobres,
que nos pides que seamos la voz de los «sin voz»,
te rogamos
por los que han sufrido las injusticias de la guerra y la codicia

De lo profundo de nuestro ser clamamos a ti, Señor.

Oye nuestro clamor, escucha nuestras oraciones.

Por los habitantes de Hiroshima y Nagasaki,
    Bikini y Eniwetok,
    Kwajalein y Mururoa,
    Fangataufa y la isla Christmas,
    la isla Johnson y Monte Bello,
    Emu y Maralinga:
Por los pueblos del Pacífico que han visto su bella tierra y su mar devastados
por explosiones nucleares.

De lo profundo de nuestro ser clamamos a ti, Señor.

Oye nuestro clamor, escucha nuestras oraciones.

Por los que, a causa de las radiaciones atómicas, sufren hoy en día
enfermedades, malformaciones genéticas y la pérdida de sus seres
queridos.
Que el dolor de sus cuerpos no quebrante sus espíritus.

De lo profundo de nuestro ser clamamos a ti, Señor.

Oye nuestro clamor, escucha nuestras oraciones.

Por los que ven hoy sus tierras y mares amenazados por la
contaminación radioactiva, a causa del depósito de desechos nucleares
y del paso de barcos nucleares.
Presérvales su salud y sus medios de existencia
y haz que puedan vivir en paz y esperanza.

De lo profundo de nuestro ser clamamos a ti, Señor.

Oye nuestro clamor, escucha nuestras oraciones.

Que tu promesa de justicia se haga realidad para aquellos por quienes rogamos.
Que puedan liberarse para vivir con amor y libertad.

De lo profundo de nuestro ser clamamos a ti, Señor.

Oye nuestro clamor, escucha nuestras oraciones,
porque eres misericordioso, y eres también
el que debemos temer, el que perdona,
el que fortifica, y el que conforta. Amen.

Life in its fullness
La vie dans sa plénitude
Leben in seiner ganzen Fülle
La vida en su plenitud

Life in its fullness
La vie dans sa plénitude
Leben in seiner ganzen Fülle
La vida en su plenitud

I. Biblical affirmations ● ***Affirmations bibliques***
   Biblische Leitsätze ● *Afirmaciones bíblicas*

17

a) For with thee is the fountain of life;
   in thy light do we see light (Psalm 36:9, RSV).

b) For the earth shall be full of the knowledge of the Lord
   as the waters cover the sea (Isaiah 11:9, RSV)

c) I have come in order that they might have life —
   life in all its fullness (John 10: 10b, TEV).

d) Our theme is the word of life. This life was made visible; we
   have seen it and bear our testimony; we here declare to you the
   eternal life that dwelt with the Father and was made visible to
   us (1 John 1:2, NEB).

II. Scripture passages ● ***Extraits de l'Ecriture***
   Bibelstellen ● *Pasajes de la Sagrada Escritura*

18

Psalm 84:   Longing for God
Deuteronomy 8:11-20:   Remember your God

The seven gifts of the Holy Spirit ● *Les sept dons de l'Esprit Saint* ● Die sieben Gaben des
Heiligen Geistes ● *Los siete dones del Espíritu Santo*

The cross of the cooperativa "La Semilla de Dios" ● *La croix, Coopérative «La Semilla de Dios*
   ● Kreuz, hergestellt in der Kooperative «La Semilla de Dios» ● *La cruz de la Cooperativa
La Semilla de Dios»

Isaiah 2:1-4:   The promise of peace
Luke 4:16-21:   The good news of the kingdom
Ephesians 3:14-21:   Fullness of life
Colossians 2:6-10:   Abounding in thanksgiving.

III. Responsive readings and litanies ● *Répons et litanies*
Responsorien und Litaneien ● *Responsorios y letanías*

19   *Of his fullness*

In the beginning God created the heaven and the earth.
The earth was without form and void, and darkness was upon
the face of the deep... And God said, "Let there be light";
and there was light... And God saw everything that he had made,
and behold, it was very good.

John 1:16   Dawn Ross, Canada

From_ his full- ness have we all_ re - ceived, grace up - on _ grace.

And the Word became flesh and dwelt among us,
full of grace and truth; we beheld his glory,
glory as of the only son from the Father.
From his fullness have we all received, grace upon grace.

Therefore if anyone is in Christ, he/she is a new creation;
the old has passed away, behold the new has come.
And all this is from God, who through Christ reconciled us
to himself and gave us the ministry of reconciliation.
From his fullness have we all received, grace upon grace.

For freedom Christ has set us free; stand fast therefore and
do not submit again to the yoke of slavery... If we live by
the Spirit, let us also walk by the Spirit.
From his fullness have we all received, grace upon grace.

19   *De sa plénitude*

Lorsque Dieu commença la création du ciel et de la terre, la
terre était déserte et vide et la ténèbre à la surface de
l'abime; le souffle de Dieu planait à la surface des eaux...

44

et Dieu dit «Que la lumière soit!» Et la lumière fut. Dieu vit
tout ce qu'il avait fait. Voilà c'était très bon.

De sa plénitude, nous avons tout reçu, et grâce sur grâce.

Et le Verbe s'est fait chair, il a demeuré parmi nous, et
nous avons vu sa gloire, gloire que le Fils unique tient du Père,
plein de grâce et de vérité.

De sa plénitude, nous avons tout reçu, et grâce sur grâce.

Aussi, si quelqu'un est en Christ, il est une nouvelle créature.
Le monde ancien est passé, voici qu'une réalité nouvelle est là.
Tout vient de Dieu, qui nous a réconciliés avec lui par le Christ
et nous a confié le ministère de la réconciliation.

De sa plénitude, nous avons tout reçu, et grâce sur grâce.

Pour que nous soyons vraiment libres, le Christ nous a libérés.
Tenez donc ferme et ne vous laissez pas remettre sous le joug de
l'esclavage... Si nous vivons par l'Esprit, marchons aussi par l'Esprit.

De sa plénitude, nous avons tout reçu, et grâce sur grâce.

19 *De su plenitud*

En el comienzo de todo, Dios creó el cielo y la tierra.
La tierra no tenía entonces ninguna forma; todo era un mar profundo
cubierto de oscuridad, y el espíritu de Dios se movía sobre el agua.
Entonces Dios dijo: «Que haya luz»! Y hubo luz...
y vió Dios que todo lo que había hecho estaba muy bien.
De ese modo se completó el sexto día.

De su plenitud recibimos todos, y gracia sobre gracia.

Y el Verbo se hizo carne y habitó entre nosotros,
lleno de gracia y de verdad; y vimos su gloria,
gloria como del Unigénito del Padre.

De su plenitud recibimos todos, y gracia sobre gracia

Por lo tanto, el que está unido a Cristo es una nueva persona.
Las cosas viejas pasaron; lo que ahora hay, es nuevo.
Todo esto es la obra de Dios, quien por medio de Cristo
nos puso en paz consigo mismo y nos dió el encargo
de poner a todos en paz con él.

De su plenitud recibimos todos, y gracia sobre gracia.

Para que seamos libres Cristo nos ha liberado; estad pues firmes
y no estéis otra vez sujetos al yugo de esclavitud... Si
vivimos por el Espíritu, andemos también por el Espíritu.

De su plenitud recibimos todos, gracia sobre gracia.

20   *Love that passes knowledge*

MAY CHRIST DWELL IN OUR HEARTS THROUGH FAITH;
MAY WE EXPERIENCE CHRIST'S LOVE WHICH SURPASSES ALL KNOWLEDGE;
MAY WE ATTAIN TO THE FULLNESS OF GOD.

Happy are those whose hearts are set upon the pilgrimage!
The Lord withholds no good thing from those who walk in sincerity.

MAY CHRIST DWELL IN OUR HEARTS THROUGH FAITH;
MAY WE EXPERIENCE CHRIST'S LOVE WHICH SURPASSES ALL KNOWLEDGE;
MAY WE ATTAIN TO THE FULLNESS OF GOD.

Obey the commandments of the Lord, love him, walk in his ways.
Choose life, that you and your descendants may live.
Heed his voice and hold fast to him.

MAY CHRIST DWELL IN OUR HEARTS THROUGH FAITH;
MAY WE EXPERIENCE CHRIST'S LOVE WHICH SURPASSES ALL KNOWLEDGE;
MAY WE ATTAIN TO THE FULLNESS OF GOD.

Your light shall break forth like the dawn,
your wound shall quickly be healed.
You shall cry for help and the Lord will answer.
He will renew your strength and you shall be like a spring
whose water never fails.

MAY CHRIST DWELL IN OUR HEARTS THROUGH FAITH;
MAY WE EXPERIENCE CHRIST'S LOVE WHICH SURPASSES ALL KNOWLEDGE;
MAY WE ATTAIN TO THE FULLNESS OF GOD.

Bring glad tidings to the poor,
proclaim liberty to captives,
restore sight to the blind, release the prisoners,
announce a year of favour from the Lord.

MAY CHRIST DWELL IN OUR HEARTS THROUGH FAITH;
MAY WE EXPERIENCE CHRIST'S LOVE WHICH SURPASSES ALL KNOWLEDGE;
MAY WE ATTAIN TO THE FULLNESS OF GOD.

They will come from the east and the west, the north and the south
and will take their place at the feast in the kingdom of God.

MAY CHRIST DWELL IN OUR HEARTS THROUGH FAITH;
MAY WE EXPERIENCE CHRIST'S LOVE WHICH SURPASSES ALL KNOWLEDGE;
MAY WE ATTAIN TO THE FULLNESS OF GOD.

20 *Wir bitten, daß Christus in unseren Herzen wohnt*

WIR BITTEN, DASS CHRISTUS IN UNSEREN HERZEN WOHNT;
DASS WIR CHRISTI LIEBE ERFAHREN, DIE ALLES WISSEN
DIESER WELT ÜBERSTEIGT;
DASS WIR ZU DER FÜLLE GOTTES GELANGEN.

Glücklich sind die, die ihr Leben wie Pilger führen.
Der Herr wird denen Gutes geben, die aufrichtig leben.

WIR BITTEN, DASS CHRISTUS IN UNSEREN HERZEN WOHNT;
DASS WIR CHRISTI LIEBE ERFAHREN, DIE ALLES WISSEN
DIESER WELT ÜBERSTEIGT;
DASS WIR ZU DER FÜLLE GOTTES GELANGEN.

Folge den Geboten des Herrn, liebe ihn, gehe seinen Weg.
Wähle das Leben, damit du und deine Nachkommen Leben haben.
Höre auf Gottes Stimme und halte fest an ihm.

WIR BITTEN, DASS CHRISTUS IN UNSEREN HERZEN WOHNT;
DASS WIR CHRISTI LIEBE ERFAHREN, DIE ALLES WISSEN
DIESER WELT ÜBERSTEIGT;
DASS WIR ZU DER FÜLLE GOTTES GELANGEN.

Licht wird aus dir hervorbrechen wie bei der Morgendämmerung,
deine Wunden werden rasch geheilt werden.
Du wirst um Hilfe rufen, und der Herr wird antworten.
Er wird deine Kraft erneuern, und du wirst einer Quelle gleichen,
deren Strom nie versiegt.

WIR BITTEN, DASS CHRISTUS IN UNSEREN HERZEN WOHNT;
DASS WIR CHRISTI LIEBE ERFAHREN, DIE ALLES WISSEN
DIESER WELT ÜBERSTEIGT;
DASS WIR ZU DER FÜLLE GOTTES GELANGEN.

Bringe frohe Botschaft den Armen,
verkündige Freiheit den Unterdrückten,
laß die Blinden wieder sehen, befreie die Gefangenen,
verkündige ein gnadenvolles Jahr des Herrn.

WIR BITTEN, DASS CHRISTUS IN UNSEREN HERZEN WOHNT;
DASS WIR CHRISTI LIEBE ERFAHREN, DIE ALLES WISSEN
DIESER WELT ÜBERSTEIGT;
DASS WIR ZU DER FÜLLE GOTTES GELANGEN.

Sie werden von Osten und Westen, von Norden und Süden kommen,
und sie werden zu Tische sitzen im Reiche Gottes.

WIR BITTEN, DASS CHRISTUS IN UNSEREN HERZEN WOHNT;
DASS WIR CHRISTI LIEBE ERFAHREN, DIE ALLES WISSEN
DIESER WELT ÜBERSTEIGT;
DASS WIR ZU DER FÜLLE GOTTES GELANGEN.

20 *El amor que transmite conocimiento*

HABITE CRISTO POR LA FE EN NUESTROS CORAZONES
PARA QUE PODAMOS EXPERIMENTAR EL AMOR DE DIOS QUE
EXCEDE A TODO CONOCIMIENTO;
PARA QUE SEAMOS LLENOS DE LA PLENITUD DE DIOS.

Dichosos aquellos cuyos corazones están prontos para
iniciar el peregrinaje!
El Señor no quitará el bien a los que andan en integridad.

HABITE CRISTO POR LA FE EN NUESTROS CORAZONES
PARA QUE PODAMOS EXPERIMENTAR EL AMOR DE DIOS QUE
EXCEDE A TODO CONOCIMIENTO;
PARA QUE SEAMOS LLENOS DE LA PLENITUD DE DIOS.

Obedece los mandamientos del Señor, ámale, anda en sus
caminos.
Escoge la vida, para que tú y tus descendientes puedan
vivir.
Oye su voz y aférrate a El.

HABITE CRISTO POR LA FE EN NUESTROS CORAZONES
PARA QUE PODAMOS EXPERIMENTAR EL AMOR DE DIOS QUE
EXCEDE A TODO CONOCIMIENTO;
PARA QUE SEAMOS LLENOS DE LA PLENITUD DE DIOS.

Entonces brotará tu luz como la aurora.
Y tu herida se curará rápidamente.
Entonces clamarás y el Señor te responderá.
El renovará tu fortaleza y serás como una fuente
cuyas aguas nunca faltan.

HABITE CRISTO POR LA FE EN NUESTROS CORAZONES
PARA QUE PODAMOS EXPERIMENTAR EL AMOR DE DIOS QUE
EXCEDE A TODO CONOCIMIENTO;
PARA QUE SEAMOS LLENOS DE LA PLENITUD DE DIOS.

Anunciad la buena nueva a los pobres,
Pregonad a los cautivos la liberación,
Restaurad la vista a los ciegos, liberad los prisioneros,
Proclamad un año de gracia del Señor.

HABITE CRISTO POR LA FE EN NUESTROS CORAZONES
PARA QUE PODAMOS EXPERIMENTAR EL AMOR DE DIOS QUE
EXCEDE A TODO CONOCIMIENTO;
PARA QUE SEAMOS LLENOS DE LA PLENITUD DE DIOS.

Vendrán del oriente y del occidente, del norte y del sur
Y se sentarán a la mesa en el Reino de Dios.

HABITE CRISTO POR LA FE EN NUESTROS CORAZONES
PARA QUE PODAMOS EXPERIMENTAR EL AMOR DE DIOS QUE
EXCEDE A TODO CONOCIMIENTO;
PARA QUE SEAMOS LLENOS DE LA PLENITUD DE DIOS.

21 *For discipleship*

O Lord our God, we thank you for
the many people throughout the ages
who have followed your way of life joyfully:
for the many saints and martyrs, men and women,
who have offered up their very lives,
so that your life abundant
may become manifest
and your kingdom may advance.

For your love and faithfulness
we will at all times praise your name.

O Lord, we thank you for those
who chose the way of your Son,
our brother Jesus Christ.
In the midst of trial, they held out hope;
in the midst of hatred, they kindled love;
in the midst of persecutions they witnessed to your power;
in the midst of despair they clung to your promise.

For your love and faithfulness
we will at all times praise your name.

O Lord, we thank you for the truth they learned and passed on to us:
that it is by giving that we shall receive;
it is by becoming weak that we shall be strong;
it is by loving others that we shall be loved;
it is by offering ourselves that the kingdom will unfold;
it is by dying that we shall inherit life everlasting.
Lord, give us courage to follow your way of life.

For your love and faithfulness
we will at all times praise your name.

21   *Für die Nachfolge Christi*

Herr, unser Gott, wir danken dir
für die vielen Menschen zu allen Zeiten,
die voller Freude deinen Weg des Lebens gegangen sind;
für die vielen Heiligen und Märtyrer,
Frauen und Männer,
die ihr Leben geopfert haben,
damit dein Leben in seiner Fülle aufleuchte,
damit dein Reich sich entfalte.

Für deine Liebe und Treue
wollen wir deinen Namen preisen immerdar.

Herr, wir danken dir für die,
die den Weg deines Sohnes gewählt haben,
den Weg unseres Bruders, Jesus Christus.
Hoffnung haben sie behalten inmitten der Angst.
Liebe haben sie entzündet inmitten des Hasses.
Deine Macht haben sie bezeugt inmitten der Vefolgung.
Deiner Verheissung haben sie geglaubt inmitten der
      Verzweiflung.

Für deine Liebe und Treue
wollen wir deinen Namen preisen immerdar.

Herr, wir danken dir für die Wahrheit, die sie erfahren
      und uns weitergegeben haben:
Nur wenn wir selbst schenken, werden wir beschenkt.
Nur wenn wir schwach werden, erwächst uns Kraft.
Nur wenn wir andere lieben, werden wir geliebt.
Nur wenn wir unser ganzes Leben einsetzen, erblüht
      Gottes Reich.
Nur wenn wir sterben, werden wir das ewige Leben erben.

Für deine Liebe und Treue
wollen wir deinen Namen preisen immerdar.

50

21   *Para el discipulado*

Oh Señor Dios nuestro, te damos gracias por
las numerosas personas que en todos los tiempos
han seguido con alegría tu camino de vida:
por todos los santos y mártires, hombres y mujeres
que han ofrecido sus propias vidas,
a fin de que tu vida de abundancia
pueda manifestarse
y tu reino pueda extenderse.

Por tu amor y fidelidad
alabaremos siempre tu nombre.

Oh Señor, te damos gracias por aquellos que
escogieron el camino de tu Hijo,
nuestro hermano Jesucristo.
En medio del infortunio, conservaron la esperanza;
en medio del odio, mantuvieron la llama del amor;
en medio de las persecuciones dieron testimonio de tu poder;
en medio de la desesperación se aferraron a tu promesa.

Por tu amor y fidelidad
alabaremos siempre tu nombre.

Oh Señor, te damos gracias por la verdad que aprendieron y
      nos comunicaron:
que si damos recibiremos;
si nos hacemos débiles, seremos fuertes;
si amamos a los demás, seremos amados;
si nos ofrecemos, el Reino se nos revelará;
que al morir, heredaremos la vida eterna.
Señor, danos fuerzas para seguir tu camino de vida.

Por tu amor y fidelidad
alabaremos siempre tu nombre.

IV. **Prayers** ● *Prières*
     Gebete ● *Oraciones*

22   *After the manner of the Lord's Prayer*

Let us, in fellowship with Christian people of all nations join in
united petition to the one God and Parent of all humankind, after
the manner of the prayer which our Lord himself has taught us.

Our Father in heaven.

We are weak and blind and selfish; but you are wisdom and love and life, and give wisdom, love and life in all its fullness to those who trust in you:

Our Father in heaven.

Through the continued search for fullness of life for all people, regardless of race and ideology:

Hallowed be your name.

Through the persistent desire in all people to seek fellowship with one another in your one family:

Hallowed be your name.

By the faithfulness of your people in seeking first your kingdom and your righteousness:

Your kingdom come.

By the new dedication of churches in all lands to the establishment of justice in all the earth:

Your kingdom come.

In the struggle against all that diminishes life in our world:

Your will be done.

In the determination among all to work for secure peace in a world order that is fair to the generations yet to be:

Your will be done.

By the establishment of peace and the unremitting search for justice:

Give us today our daily bread.

By passionate caring and committed sharing:

Give us today our daily bread.

Because by our self-interest and self-concern we have increased the bitterness between peoples and nations:

Forgive us our sins.

Because we have been arrogant, seeking to exalt ourselves rather than to find your will for us and do it:

Forgive us our sins.

If other countries while pursuing their own interests have hindered ours and impoverished the life of our people:
We forgive those who sin against us.

If any have injured us by exploiting our ignorance and weakness:
We forgive those who sin against us.

When opportunity comes to secure better living standards for ourselves at the cost of increased poverty to others:
Save us from the time of trial.

When fear distracts the mind or security lulls the conscience, and we are in danger of forgetting you:
Save us from the time of trial.

At times of self-satisfaction, self-seeking and self-confidence:
Deliver us from evil.

When we fear the designs of others, and desire to gain security or advantage by unjust means:
Deliver us from evil.

For over all races and nations you rule as sovereign; your parental love embraces all; and in your will is our peace and in your life our life.
For the kingdom, the power and the glory are yours, now and forever. Amen.

22   *Sur le modèle du Notre Père*

En communion avec les chrétiens de toutes nations, unissons notre prière au Dieu unique et Père de toute l'humanité, selon le modèle de la prière que notre Seigneur lui-même nous a enseignée:
Notre Père, qui es aux cieux.

Nous sommes faibles, aveugles, égoïstes; mais tu es sagesse, amour et vie, et tu donnes la sagesse, l'amour et la vie en toute sa plénitude à ceux qui ont confiance en toi:
Notre Père, qui es aux cieux.

A travers la recherche continue d'une plénitude de vie pour tous, sans tenir compte des races et des opinions:
Que ton nom soit sanctifié.

A travers le désir persistant chez tous les êtres de chercher la communion les uns avec les autres dans ton unique famille:

Que ton nom soit sanctifié.

En la fidélité de ton peuple à chercher d'abord ton Royaume et ta justice:

Que ton règne vienne.

Par la consécration nouvelle des Eglises, en tous pays, à l'établissement de la justice sur toute la terre:

Que ton règne vienne.

Dans le combat contre tout ce qui amoindrit la vie en notre monde:

Que ta volonté soit faite.

Pentecost • *Pentecôte* • Pfingsten • *Pentecostés*

1965   SADAO WATANABE

Dans la détermination de chacun à travailler pour une paix assurée au sein d'un ordre mondial qui soit bon pour les générations à venir:

Que ta volonté soit faite.

Par l'établissement de la paix et la recherche inlassable de la justice:

Donne-nous aujourd'hui notre pain de ce jour.

Par la passion de servir et l'engagement à partager:

Donne-nous aujourd'hui notre pain de ce jour.

Parce que nous avons augmenté l'amertume entre peuples et nations, par notre égoïsme et la préoccupation de nous-mêmes.

Pardonne-nous nos offenses.

Parce que nous avons été arrogant, cherchant plus à nous élever nous-mêmes qu'à découvrir ta volonté pour nous et à l'accomplir:

Pardonne-nous nos offenses.

Si d'autres pays, poursuivant leurs propres intérêts, ont empêché l'épanouissement des nôtres et appauvri la vie de notre peuple:

Nous pardonnons à ceux qui nous ont offensés.

Si quelques-uns nous ont fait du tort en profitant de notre ignorance ou de notre faiblesse:

Nous pardonnons à ceux qui nous ont offensés.

Quand l'occasion se présente de nous assurer un meilleur standard de vie au prix d'une pauvreté accrue pour les autres:

Ne nous soumets pas à la tentation.

Quand la peur affole notre esprit ou que la sécurité endort notre conscience, et que nous courons le danger de t'oublier:

Ne nous soumets pas à la tentation.

Aux moments de satisfaction de soi, de recherche de soi et de confiance en soi:

Délivre-nous du mal.

Aux moments de crainte concernant les intentions des autres et de désir d'obtenir sécurité et avantages par des moyens injustes:

Délivre-nous du mal.

Car tu gouvernes en souverain toutes les races et nations; ton amour paternel les embrasse toutes; dans ta volonté est notre paix et dans ta vie notre vie.

A toi le règne, la puissance et la gloire,
pour les siècles des siècles. Amen.

23 *Grant us wholeness*

Eternal God, as you created humankind in your image,
women and men, male and female, renew us in that image:

God the Holy Spirit, by your strength and love
comfort us as those whom a mother comforts:

Lord Jesus Christ, by your death and resurrection,
give us the joy of those for whom pain and suffering become,
in hope, the fruitful agony of travail:

God the Holy Trinity, grant that we may together
enter into new life, your promised rest of achievement
and fulfilment—world without end. Amen.

23 *Donne-nous la plénitude*

Dieu éternel, qui as créé l'humanité à ton image, femmes et hommes,
renouvelle-nous à cette image.

Dieu, Saint-Esprit, par ta force et ton amour,
réconforte-nous comme une mère qui console.

Seigneur Jésus-Christ, par ta mort et ta résurrection,
donne-nous la joie de ceux pour qui la douleur et la souffrance
deviennent, dans l'espérance, la douleur fructueuse de l'enfantement.

Dieu, sainte Trinité, fais que nous puissions entrer ensemble dans
la vie nouvelle, le repos promis où tout est achevé et accompli,
pour les siècles des siècles. Amen.

23   *Schenke uns Ganzheit*

Ewiger Gott, der Du die Menschen nach Deinem Bilde geschaffen hast,
Frauen und Männer, männlich und weiblich,
erneuere uns nach diesem Bilde;

Gott, Heiliger Geist, tröste uns durch Deine Kraft und Liebe,
so wie uns eine Mutter tröstet;

Herr Jesus Christus, gib uns durch Deinen Tod und Deine Auferstehung
die Freude derer, für die Schmerzen und Leiden
zu hoffnungsvollen, fruchtbaren Geburtswehen werden;

Gott, heilige Dreieinigkeit, schenke uns, dass wir gemeinsam in ein
neues Leben treten: Deine verheissene Vollendung und Erfüllung
— Welt ohne Ende. Amen.

24   *Aus einem Fürbittgebet von Eltern behinderter Kinder*

Herr, gleichzeitig empfinden wir viel Freude durch unsere behinderten
Kinder:
— Freude über jede Reaktion, die wir nicht vermutet haben,
— Freude über ihre Zuneigung, jedes Wort oder jede Geste, die an
   uns gerichtet sind,
— Freude über die gemeinsamen Erlebnisse mit ihnen.
Herr, wir danken Dir, dass sich unsere Kinder, manchmal sogar
mehr als wir Eltern, über die einfachsten Dinge freuen können.
Hierfür und für das, was sie uns bedeuten, danken wir Dir, o Herr.

24   *From a prayer by parents of handicapped children*

Lord, though disabled, our children with handicaps are a source of
great joy to us:
— joy in every response we had not expected
— joy in their affectionate ways, every word and gesture meant for us
— joy in the experiences we share with them.
We thank you, Lord, that very often our children are more able
than we are to rejoice in the simplest things.
For this and all that they mean to us, we thank you, Lord.

24 *Tomado de una oración de padres de niños impedidos*

Señor, aunque nuestros hijos están impedidos son fuente de gran alegría para nosotros:
— alegría en cada reacción que no nos esperábamos,
— alegría en sus muestras de afección hacia nosotros, sus palabras o sus gestos.
— alegría cada vez que compartimos algo con ellos.
Te damos gracias, Señor, porque muchas veces nuestros hijos son mas capaces que nosotros, de alegrarse con las cosas más sencillas. Por ello, y por todo lo que significan para nosotros, te damos gracias. Señor.

25 *In unison with all creatures*

O God, our God: You have brought all spiritual and rational powers into being for the sake of obeying your will. We beseech you to accept the hymns which we, in unison with all your creatures, sing to your glory as best we can. Reward us with the overflowing graces of your bounty, for every creature in heaven, on earth, and below the earth bows down before you, and every creature sings of your ineffable glory. You are the only true and all merciful God, and all the powers of heaven praise you; and we glorify you, Father, Son and Holy Spirit, now and ever, and forever. Amen.

25 *A l'unisson, avec toutes tes créatures*

Dieu, notre Dieu, tu as créé tous les pouvoirs de l'esprit et de l'intelligence afin qu'ils obéissent à ta volonté. Nous te supplions d'accepter les louanges qu'avec toutes les créatures nous chantons pour te glorifier autant qu'il est possible. Récompense-nous des grâces infinies de ta bonté, car toute créature, au ciel, sur terre et sous la terre, se prosterne devant toi et chante ta gloire ineffable. Tu es le seul vrai Dieu de miséricorde infinie; toutes les puissances des cieux te louent et nous te glorifions, Père, Fils et Saint-Esprit, maintenant et toujours, pour les siècles des siècles. Amen.

25 *Im Einklang mit aller Kreatur*

Herr, unser Gott: Du hast alle geistigen und vernünftigen Mächte ins Leben gerufen, damit sie Deinem Willen gehorchen. Wir bitten Dich, nimm unsere Lieder an, die wir im Einklang mit all Deinen Geschöpfen zu Deiner Ehre singen, so gut wir können. Beschenke uns mit der überschwenglichen Gnade Deiner Wohltaten, denn alle Kreatur im Himmel, auf Erden und unter der Erde neigt sich vor Dir, und alle Kreatur singt von Deinem unaussprechlichen Ruhm. Du bist der einzig wahre und barmherzige Gott, und alle Mächte des Himmels preisen Dich; wir rühmen Dich, Vater, Sohn und Heiliger Geist, jetzt und von Ewigkeit zu Ewigkeit. Amen.

Life in unity
La vie dans l'unité
Leben in Einheit
La vida en la unidad

Hozanna, by John Coburn • *Hosanna, de John Coburn* • Hosianna, von John Coburn • *Hosanna, de John Coburn*

Life in unity
La vie dans l'unité
Leben in Einheit
La vida en la unidad

I. Biblical affirmations ● *Affirmations bibliques*
Biblische Leitsätze ● *Afirmaciones bíblicas*

26

a) O that you had harkened to my commandments!
   Then your peace would have been like a river
   and your righteousness like the waves of the sea (Isaiah 48:18, RSV).

b) And they shall beat their swords into plowshares
   and their spears into pruning hooks;
   nations shall not lift up sword against nation,
   neither shall they learn war anymore (Isaiah 2:4, RSV).

c) May they be in us, just as you are in me and I am in you.
   May they be one, so that the world will believe that you sent me
   (John 17: 21b, TEV).

d) And to all these qualities add love, which binds all things
   together in perfect unity (Colossians 3:14, TEV).

II. Scripture passages ● *Extraits de l'Ecriture*
Bibelstellen ● *Pasajes de la Sagrada Escritura*

27

Isaiah 42: 5-9:   Covenant with all peoples.
       51: 1-6:   The one source

Acts 2: 43-47:   Life among believers
I Corinthians 10:16-17: The one bread.
Galatians 3: 27-28:   The broken barriers.
Ephesians 4: 3-6:   One in Christ,

III. Responsive readings and litanies ● *Répons et litanies*
Responsorien und Litaneien ● *Responsorios y letanías*

28   *Grant us peace and unity*

Dear friends, let us love one another, because love comes from God.
Whoever loves is a child of God and knows God.

Jesus Christ, the life of the world, and of all creation,
Forgive our separation and grant us peace and unity. (sung)

The peace that Christ gives is to guide you in the
decisions you make; for it is to this peace that God
has called you together in the one body.

Jesus Christ, the life of the world, and of all creation,
Forgive our separation and grant us peace and unity.

With his own body he broke down the wall that separated them...
By his death on the cross Christ destroyed their enmity...

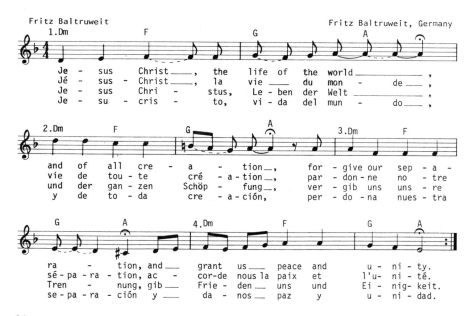

Fritz Baltruweit   Fritz Baltruweit, Germany

64

by means of the cross he united both races into one body...
In union with him you too are being built together with all others
into a place where God lives through his Spirit.

Jesus Christ, the life of the world, and of all creation,
Forgive our separation and grant us peace and unity.

Do your best to preserve the unity which the Spirit gives by means
of the peace that binds you together. There is one body, one spirit,
just as there is one hope to which God has called you.

Jesus Christ, the life of the world, and of all creation,
Forgive our separation and grant us peace and unity.

THERE IS ONE LORD, ONE FAITH, ONE BAPTISM; THERE IS ONE GOD
WHO IS LORD OF ALL, WORKS THROUGH ALL AND IN ALL. AMEN.

28   *Donne-nous la paix et l'unité*

Mes biens-aimés, aimons-nous les uns les autres, car l'amour
vient de Dieu, et quiconque aime est né de Dieu et parvient
à la connaissance de Dieu

Jésus Christ, la vie du monde, vie de toute création,
pardonne notre séparation, accorde-nous la paix et l'unité. (chanté)

La paix que le Christ donne doit vous guider dans vos
décisions; car c'est à cette paix que Dieu vous a tous
appelés en un seul corps.

Jésus Christ, la vie du monde, vie de toute céation,
pardonne notre séparation, accorde-nous la paix et l'unité.

Dans sa chair, il a détruit le mur de séparation... Par sa
mort sur la croix, le Christ a détruit leur hostilité...;
au moyen de la croix, il a uni les deux races en un
seul corps... C'est en lui que vous aussi, vous êtes
ensemble intégrés à la construction pour devenir une demeure
de Dieu par l'Esprit.

Jésus Christ, la vie du monde, vie de toute création
pardonne notre séparation, accorde-nous la paix et l'unité.

Appliquez-vous à garder l'unité de l'esprit par le lien
de la paix. Il y a un seul corps et un seul Esprit, de
même que votre vocation vous a appelés à une seule espérance.

Jésus Christ, la vie du monde, vie de toute création,
pardonne notre séparation, accorde-nous la paix et l'unité.

UN SEUL SEIGNEUR, UNE SEULE FOI, UN SEUL BAPTÊME; UN SEUL
DIEU QUI RÈGNE SUR TOUS, AGIT PAR TOUS,
ET DEMEURE EN TOUS. AMEN.

28   Schenke uns Frieden und Einheit

Ihr Lieben, lasst uns einander liebhaben, denn die Liebe ist von
Gott, und wer liebhat, der ist von Gott geboren und kennt Gott.

*Jesus Christus, Leben der Welt und der ganzen Schöpfung, vergib
uns unsre Trennung, gib Frieden uns und Einigkeit.* (gesungen)

Der Friede Christi leite euch in euren Entscheidungen; denn zu
diesem Frieden hat Gott euch in einem Leib berufen.

*Jesus Christus, Leben der Welt und der ganzen Schöpfung, vergib
uns unsre Trennung, gib Frieden uns und Einigkeit.*

Mit seinem eigenen Leib hat er die Mauer niedergerissen, die sie
trennte... Durch seinen Tod am Kreuz hat Christus ihre Feindschaft
zunichte gemacht... Durch das Kreuz hat er beide (Juden und
Heiden) in einem Leib vereint... Durch ihn werdet auch ihr mit
allen anderen zusammen erbaut zu einer Wohnung, wo Gott durch
seinen Geist lebt.

*Jesus Christus, Leben der Welt und der ganzen Schöpfung, vergib
uns unsre Trennung, gib Frieden uns und Einigkeit.*

Seid fleissig, zu halten die Einigkeit im Geist durch das Band des
Friedens: *ein* Leib und *ein* Geist, wie ihr auch berufen seid zu *einer*
Hoffnung.

*Jesus Christus, Leben der Welt und der ganzen Schöpfung, vergib
uns unsre Trennung, gib Frieden uns und Einigkeit.*

EIN HERR, EIN GLAUBE, EINE TAUFE; EIN GOTT, DER DA IST ÜBER
ALLEN UND DURCH ALLE UND IN ALLEN. AMEN.

29   Make us one

(Prayers for unity—from many countries)

O Lord Jesus, stretch forth thy wounded hands
in blessing over thy people, to heal and to
restore, and to draw them to thyself and to
one another in love.

(Middle East)

O God, thou art one; make us one.

O God, forgive us for bringing this stumbling block of
disunity to a people who want to belong to one family.
The church for which our Saviour died is broken, and people
can scarcely believe that we hold one faith and follow one Lord.
O Lord, bring about the unity which thou hast promised,
not tomorrow or the next day, but today.

(Africa)

O God, thou art one; make us one.

O Lord, forgive the sins of thy servants. May we banish
from our minds all disunion and strife; may our souls be cleansed
of all hatred and malice towards others, and may we receive the
fellowship of the Holy Meal in oneness of mind and peace with one
another.

(India)

O God, thou art one; make us one.

Just as the bread which we break was scattered over the earth,
was gathered in and became one,
bring us together from everywhere into the kingdom of your peace.

(Epistle to Diognetus)

O God, thou art one; make us one.

29 *Fais que nous soyons un*

(Prières de divers pays pour l'unité)

Seigneur Jésus, étends tes mains blessées pour répandre
ta bénédiction sur ton peuple, pour guérir et restaurer,
pour attirer les tiens à toi et les rapprocher les uns
des autres dans l'amour.

(Moyen Orient)

Dieu qui es un, fais que nous soyons un.

O Dieu, pardonne-nous d'apporter la désunion à un peuple
qui veut ne faire qu'une seule famille. L'Eglise pour
laquelle notre Sauveur est mort est divisée, et l'on a du
mal à croire que nous proclamons la même foi et suivons le
même Seigneur.
Seigneur, donne-nous l'unité que tu as promise non pas
demain ou après demain, mais aujourd'hui.

(Afrique)

Dieu qui es un, fais que nous soyons un.

Seigneur, pardonne les fautes de tes serviteurs. Donne-nous
de bannir de notre esprit toute discorde et querelle, de
purifier nos âmes de toute haine et malveillance à l'égard
d'autrui, et de recevoir la communion de la Sainte Cène dans
l'unité de l'esprit et en paix les uns avec les autres.

(Inde)

Dieu qui es un, fais que nous soyons un.

Comme le pain que nous rompons était épars sur la terre, puis
a été recueilli pour devenir un, rassemble-nous des extrêmités
de la terre pour nous conduire en ton Royaume de paix.

(Epître à Diognète)

Dieu qui es un, fais que nous soyons un.

29   *Haz que seamos uno*

(Oraciones de diversos países por la unidad)

Oh Señor Jesús, extiende tus manos heridas
para bendecir a tu pueblo, para curarlo y
restaurarlo; llévalo hacia ti y haz que
le una el amor mutuo.

(Medio Oriente)

Oh Dios, que eres uno; haz que seamos uno.

Oh Dios, perdónanos por haber aportado el obstáculo de la
desunión a un pueblo que quiere pertenecer a una misma familia.
La Iglesia por la cual nuestro Salvador murió está dividida
y apenas podemos creer que proclamamos la misma fe y seguimos
al mismo Señor.
Oh Señor, danos la unidad que nos has prometido,
dánosla hoy, sin esperar a mañana.

(Africa)

Oh Dios, que eres uno; haz que seamos uno.

Oh Señor, perdona los pecados de tus siervos. Haz que
alejemos de nuestras mentes toda desunión y discordia; que
nuestras almas se purifiquen del odio y de la maldad hacia los
demás, y que podamos recibir la comunión de la Santa Cena en
la unidad del espíritu y en la paz mutua.

(India)

Oh Dios, que eres uno; haz que seamos uno.

Al igual que el pan que rompemos fue esparcido sobre la tierra,
y después recogido para ser uno, haz que nos reunamos
desde todos los lugares de la tierra en tu reino de paz.

(Epistola a Diogneto)

Oh Dios, que eres uno; haz que seamos uno.

30   *La fiesta de la vida*

Vengan, vengan todos

¡Vengan!
Celebramos la Cena del Señor
Hagamos todos juntos un pan enorme
y preparemos mucho vino
como en las bodas de Caná

Vengan, vengan todos a la mesa del Señor.

Que las mujeres no se olviden de la sal
Que los hombres consigan levadura
Que vengan muchos invitados:
ciegos, sordos, cojos, presos, pobres

Vengan, vengan todos a este encuentro con el Señor.

¡Pronto!
Sigamos la receta del Señor
Batamos todos la masa con las manos
y veamos con alegría como crece el pan.

Vengan, vengan todos a esta celebración con nuestro Señor.

Porque hoy celebramos
el encuentro con Jesús
Hoy renovamos nuestro compromiso con el Reino:
Nadie se quedará con hambre.

Vengan, vamos a participar en la fiesta de la vida con nuestro Señor.

30   *The feast of life*

Come! O people, come!

Let us celebrate the supper of the Lord,
let us together bake a giant loaf,

69

and together prepare the jars of wine
as at the wedding feast in Cana.

Come, O people, come to the table of the Lord.

Let the women not forget the salt
Nor the men the leaven
And let us invite many guests:
the lame, the blind, the deaf, the poor.

Come, O people, come for this meeting with the Lord.

Quickly now!
Let us follow the recipe of our Lord;
Let us together knead the dough with our hands,
and watch with joy the rising bread.

Come, O people, come for this celebration with our Lord.

Because today we are celebrating
Our commitment to Christ Jesus;
Today we are renewing our commitment to the kingdom;
And no one shall go hungry away.

Come, let us participate in the feast of life with our Lord.

30   *Fest des Lebens*

Kommt, ihr Leute, kommt,

lasst uns miteinander das Mahl des Herrn feiern.
Lasst uns ein ganz grosses Brot backen,
lasst uns die Weinkrüge bereitstellen
wie bei der Hochzeit zu Kana.

Kommt, ihr Leute, kommt zum Tisch des Herrn.

Ihr Frauen, vergesst nicht das Salz,
Ihr Männer, bringt auch die Hefe dazu.
Viele Gäste sollen kommen,
die Lahmen, die Blinden, die Armen, die Behinderten.

Kommt, ihr Leute, kommt, wir werden dem Herrn begegnen.

Kommt schnell.
Wir wollen den Ratschlägen des Herrn folgen:
zusammen wollen wir den Teig kneten mit unseren Händen,
mit Freude werden wir sehen, wie das Brot wächst.

Kommt, ihr Leute, kommt zu diesem Fest mit dem Herrn.

Denn heute treffen wir ihn selbst, unsern Herrn.
Heute werden wir von neuem unser Leben hingeben
für das Reich Gottes.
Niemand soll hungrig weggehen.

Kommt, lasst uns gemeinsam das Fest des Lebens feiern
zusammen mit unseren Herrn.

IV. **Prayers** ● *Prières*
Gebete ● *Oraciones*

31 *Heal us*

Grandfather,
Look at our brokenness.

We know that in all creation
Only the human family
Has strayed from the Sacred Way.

We know that we are the ones
Who are divided
And we are the ones
Who must come back together
To walk in the Sacred Way.

Grandfather,
Sacred One,
Teach us love, compassion, and honour
That we may heal the earth
And heal each other.

31 *Guéris-nous*

Grand-Père,
Vois comme nous sommes déchirés.

Nous savons que de toute la création
Seule la famille humaine
S'est écartée de la voie sacrée.

Nous savons que nous sommes les seuls
A être divisés,

Les seuls à devoir revenir ensemble
Dans la voie sacrée.

Grand-Père,
Sacré,
Enseigne-nous l'amour, la compassion et l'honneur
Afin que nous guérissions la terre
Et nous guérissions les uns les autres.

31 *Sánanos*

Padre de nuestros padres,
Mira nuestros quebrantamientos

Sabemos que en toda la creación
solamente la familia humana
se ha descarriado del Camino Sacro.

Sabemos que somos nosotros
los únicos que estamos divididos
Y que somos nosotros
los que juntos debemos volver
a caminar por el Camino Sacro.

Padre de nuestros padres,
Santo,
Enséñanos el amor, la compasión y el honor
para que podamos sanar la tierra
y sanarnos unos a otros.

32 *For all faiths*

O God, we thank you
for the wholeness of the human family:
for people of other faiths and of none, especially those who are our
friends and neighbours;
for the rich variety of human experience and the gifts we bring to
one another when we meet in a spirit of acceptance and love;
for dialogue in community, and for mutual enrichment and growing
understanding;
for movements to establish and sustain the legitimate rights of
persons of every religious conviction.

"Adwoe", symbol of peace • *«Adwoe», symbole de paix* • «Adwoe», Symbol des
Friedens • *«Adwoe», símbolo de la paz*

And we pray to you
that people of all faiths may enjoy the freedom to set forth their
conviction with integrity and listen to one another in humility;
that the Church may perform a reconciling ministry in a world
divided by suspicion and misunderstanding, and bring healing to
those places where religious intolerance fractures human community;
that the Church may bear a true and loving witness to the One it
calls Lord, in whose name we pray. Amen.

32   *Pour toutes les religions*

O Dieu, nous te rendons grâce
pour l'ensemble de la famille humaine;
pour ceux qui professent d'autres religions ou qui n'en professent
aucune, et en particulier pour ceux qui sont nos amis et voisins;
pour l'extrême diversité des expériences humaines et pour les dons
que nous nous apportons mutuellement quand nous nous rencontrons
dans un esprit d'accueil et d'amour, pour le dialogue dans la
communauté, et pour l'enrichissement mutuel et la meilleure
compréhension qui en découlent;
pour les mouvements qui établissent et soutiennent les droits des
personnes de toutes convictions religieuses.

Et nous te prions
pour que les êtres humains, quelle que soit leur religion, puissent
être libres d'affirmer leurs convictions avec intégrité et s'écoutent
les uns les autres avec humilité;
pour que l'Eglise accomplisse un ministère de réconciliation dans
un monde divisé par la suspicion et l'incompréhension, et qu'elle
exerce une action réparatrice là où l'intolérance religieuse divise la
communauté humaine; pour que l'Eglise témoigne avec amour et
vérité de Celui qu'elle appelle Seigneur; en son nom, nous t'en
prions. Amen.

32   *Für jeden Glauben*

Herr Gott, wir danken Dir
für die ganze menschliche Familie:
für Menschen anderen und keines Glaubens,
besonders für unsere Freunde und Nachbarn;
für die reiche Vielfalt menschlicher Erfahrungen und Gaben,
die wir einander entgegenbringen, wenn wir zusammenkommen
im Geist des einander Annehmens und der Liebe;
für den Dialog in Gemeinschaft,
für gegenseitige Bereicherung und wachsendes Verständnis;

für Bewegungen, die sich für die legitimen Rechte von Personen jeder religiösen Überzeugung einsetzen und sie stärken.

Wir bitten Dich,
dass Menschen jeden Glaubens die Freiheit gewinnen,
ihre Überzeugung unbescholten zum Ausdruck zu bringen
und in Demut aufeinander zu hören;
dass die Kirche ein versöhnendes Amt ausübt in einer Welt, die durch Misstrauen und Missverständnis getrennt ist, und heilende Kraft dorthin bringt, wo religiöse Unduldsamkeit menschliche Gemeinschaft zerstört;
dass die Kirche ein wahres und liebevolles Zeugnis ablegt für den Einen, den sie Herrn nennt, und in dessen Namen wir beten. Amen.

33   Prayer for reconciliation

Across the barriers that divide race from race:
Reconcile us, O Christ, by your cross.

Across the barriers that divide the rich from the poor:
Reconcile us, O Christ, by your cross.

Across the barriers that divide people of different faiths:
Reconcile us, O Christ, by your cross.

Across the barriers that divide Christians:
Reconcile us, O Christ, by your cross.

Across the barriers that divide men and women, young and old:
Reconcile us, O Christ, by your cross.

CONFRONT US, O CHRIST, WITH THE HIDDEN PREJUDICES AND FEARS
    WHICH DENY AND BETRAY OUR PRAYERS.
    ENABLE US TO SEE THE CAUSES OF STRIFE, REMOVE FROM US ALL
    FALSE SENSE OF SUPERIORITY. TEACH US TO GROW IN UNITY
    WITH ALL GOD'S CHILDREN. AMEN.

33   Gebet um Versöhnung

Über die Schranken, die Rasse von Rasse trennen,
Versöhne uns, Christus, durch Dein Kreuz.

Über die Schranken, die Reiche von Armen trennen,
Versöhne uns, Christus, durch Dein Kreuz.

Über die Schranken, die Menschen verschiedener Religionen trennen,
Versöhne uns, Christus, durch Dein Kreuz.

Über die Schranken, die Christen untereinander trennen,
Versöhne uns, Christus, durch Dein Kreuz.

Über die Schranken, die Männer und Frauen, Jung und Alt voneinander trennen,
Versöhne uns, Christus, durch Dein Kreuz.

LASS UNS, CHRISTUS, DEN VERBORGENEN VORURTEILEN UND ÄNGSTEN
BEGEGNEN, DIE UNSERE GEBETE VERLEUGNEN UND VERRATEN.
ERMÖGLICHE ES UNS, DIE URSACHEN DES STREITES ZU ERKENNEN;
NIMM WEG VON UNS ALLE FALSCHE ÜBERLEGENHEIT. LEHRE
UNS, IN EINTRACHT MIT ALLEN KINDERN GOTTES ZU WACHSEN.
AMEN.

33 *Oración para lograr la reconciliación*

A través de las barreras que separan las razas:
Reconcílianos, oh Cristo, por tu cruz.

A través de las barreras que separan a los ricos de los pobres:
Reconcílianos, oh Cristo, por tu cruz.

A través de las barreras que separan a los fieles de diferentes religiones:
Reconcílianos, oh Cristo, por tu cruz.

A través de las barreras que dividen a los cristianos de diferentes
denominaciones y de diferentes concepciones teológicas:
Reconcílianos, oh Cristo, por tu cruz.

A través de las barreras que separan a los jóvenes de los viejos, a
los hombres se las mujeres:
Reconcílianos, oh Cristo, por tu cruz.

HAZNOS VER, OH CRISTO, LOS PREJUICIOS Y MIEDOS OCULTOS QUE
NIEGAN Y TRAICIONAN LAS ORACIONES QUE PRONUNCIAMOS.
HAZ QUE PODAMOS CONOCER LA CAUSA DE LA LUCHA; QUÍTANOS
TODO FALSO SENTIDO DE SUPERIORIDAD. ENSÉÑANOS A CRECER
EN LA UNIDAD CON TODOS LOS HIJOS DE DIOS. AMÉN.

Acts of penitence
Prières de repentance
Bussgebete
Actos de penitencia

Creeds
Confessions de foi
Glaubensbekenntnisse
Credos

Contemporary affirmations of faith
Affirmations contemporaines de la foi
Glaubensbekenntnisse der Gegenwart
Afirmaciones contemporáneas de fe

General prayers
Prières sans thème précis
Allgemeine Gebete
Oraciones varias

The return of the Prodigal Son, by Rembrandt van Rijn • *Le retour du fils prodigue, de Rembrandt van Rijn* • Die Rückkehr des verlorenen Sohnes, von Rembrandt van Rijn • *La vuelta del hijo prodigo, de Rembrandt van Rijn*

Acts of penitence
Prières de repentance
Bussgebete
Actos de penitencia

I

34   *You know us as we are*

We confess to you, Lord, what we are:
>   We are not the people we like others to think we are;
>   We are afraid to admit even to ourselves what lies in the depths of our
>   souls.
But we do not want to hide our true selves from you.
We believe that you know us as we are, and yet you love us.
Help us not to shrink from self-knowledge:
>   teach us to respect ourselves for your sake;
Give us the courage to put our trust in your guiding power.
Raise us out of the paralysis of guilt
>   into the freedom and energy of forgiven people.
And for those who through long habit
>   find forgiveness hard to accept,
>   we ask you to break their bondage and set them free,
through Jesus Christ our Lord. Amen.

34   *Tu nous connais tels que nous sommes*

Nous te confessons, Seigneur, ce que nous sommes:
>   Nous ne sommes pas ce que nous aimerions que les autres pensent de
>   nous;
>   Nous avons peur de nous avouer à nous-mêmes ce qui
>   se cache dans les profondeurs de nos âmes.
Mais nous ne voulons pas te cacher la vérité de nous-mêmes.
Nous croyons que tu nous connais tels que nous sommes,
>   et pourtant tu nous aimes.

Aide-nous à ne pas nous dérober à la connaissance de nous-mêmes:
apprends-nous à nous respecter nous-mêmes à cause de toi;
Donne-nous le courage de mettre notre confiance dans ta puissance qui
nous guide.
Relève-nous de la culpabilité qui nous paralyse,
pour nous donner la liberté et l'énergie d'un peuple pardonné.
Et brise les liens de ceux qui trouvent difficile d'accepter le pardon,
par longue habitude: rends-les libres, nous t'en prions,
par Jésus-Christ, notre Seigneur. Amen.

34 *Du weißt, wer wir sind*

Wir bekennen dir, Herr, wer wir sind:
Wir sind nicht die Menschen,
für die wir gerne gehalten werden möchten.
Wir haben Angst, auch nur uns selber einzugestehen,
was in den Tiefen unserer Seelen vor sich geht.
Aber wir wollen unser wahres Selbst vor dir nicht verbergen.
Wir sind überzeugt, dass du weißt, wer wir wirklich sind
und dass du uns trotzdem liebst.
Hilf uns, nicht zurückzuschrecken vor unserer Selbsterkenntnis.
Zeige uns, wie wir um deinetwillen uns selber neu achten können.
Gib uns den Mut, unser Vertrauen auf deine helfende Kraft zu setzen.
Hole uns heraus aus lähmender Schuld
in die Freiheit und Tatkraft derer, denen vergeben ist.
Und für alle, die durch lange Gewöhnung
es schwer haben, Vergebung anzunehmen,
bitten wir dich: zerbrich ihre Fesseln und befreie sie.
Durch Jesus Christus, unseren Herrn. Amen.

II

35 *Restore us, O Lord*

Lord God almighty,
forgive your church
its wealth among the poor,
its fear among the unjust,
its cowardice among the oppressed,

forgive us, your children,
our lack of confidence in you,
our lack of hope in your reign,
our lack of faith in your presence,
our lack of trust in your mercy.

Restore us to your covenant
	with your people;
	bring us to true repentance;
teach us to accept the sacrifice of Christ;
make us strong with the comfort of your Holy Spirit.

Break us where we are proud,
Make us where we are weak,
Shame us where we trust ourselves,
Name us where we have lost ourselves:
Through Jesus Christ our Lord. Amen.

35   *Rétablis-nous, Seigneur*

Seigneur Dieu tout-puissant,
pardonne à ton Eglise
	sa richesse au milieu des pauvres,
	sa crainte parmi les injustes,
	sa lâcheté parmi les opprimés;

pardonne à tes enfants
	leur manque d'assurance en toi,
	leur manque d'espérance en ton règne,
	leur manque de foi en ta présence,
	leur manque de confiance en ta miséricorde.

Rétablis-nous dans ton alliance
	avec ton peuple,
	conduis-nous à une vraie repentance;
apprends-nous à accepter le sacrifice du Christ,
rends-nous forts par le secours de ton Saint-Esprit.

Brise-nous lorsque nous sommes orgueilleux.
Fortifie-nous lorsque nous sommes faibles.
Humilie-nous lorsque nous comptons sur nous-mêmes.
Donne-nous un nom lorsque nous sommes perdus.
Par Jésus-Christ, notre Seigneur. Amen.

35   *Restablécenos, Señor*

Señor Dios todopoderoso,
perdona a tu iglesia
	su riqueza entre los pobres,
	su miedo entre los injustos,
	su cobardía entre los oprimidos,

perdónanos, a nosotros, tus hijos,
    nuestra falta de confianza en ti,
    nuestra falta de esperanza en tu Reino.
    nuestra falta de fe en tu presencia,
    nuestra falta de confianza en tu misericordia.

Restablécenos en tu alianza
    con tu pueblo;
    condúcenos a un arrepentimiento verdadero;
enséñanos a aceptar el sacrificio de Cristo;
danos fortaleza con la ayuda de tu Espíritu Santo.

Quebrántanos cuando somos orgullosos.
Haznos de nuevo cuando somos débiles.
Humíllanos cuando confiamos en nosotros mismos.
Danos un nombre cuando nos encontremos perdidos.
Por Jesucristo nuestro Señor. Amén.

Creeds
Confessions de foi
Glaubensbekenntnisse
Credos

I

36   *Nicene - Constantinopolitan Creed* (text of 381)

We believe in one God,
the Father, the Almighty,
maker of heaven and earth,
of all that is, seen and unseen.

We believe in one Lord, Jesus Christ,
the only Son of God,
eternally begotten of the Father,
Light from Light,
true God from true God,
begotten, not made,
of one Being with the Father:
through him all things were made.
For us and for our salvation he came down from heaven;
by the power of the Holy Spirit he became incarnate
from the Virgin Mary
and was made man.
For our sake he was crucified under Pontius Pilate;
he suffered death and was buried;
on the third day he rose again in accordance with the scriptures;
he ascended into heaven.
He is seated at the right hand of the Father,
he will come again in glory
to judge the living and the dead,
and his kingdom will have no end.

We believe in the Holy Spirit,
the Lord, the giver of life,
who proceeds from the Father;

with the Father and the Son
he is worshipped and glorified;
he has spoken through the Prophets.
We believe in one, holy, catholic and apostolic Church.
We acknowledge one baptism for the forgiveness of sins.
We look for the resurrection of the dead,
and the life of the world to come. Amen.

36   *Symbole de Nicée - Constantinople* (texte de 381)

Nous croyons en un seul Dieu,
le Père, le Tout-puissant,
Créateur du ciel et de la terre,
de toutes les choses visibles et invisibles.

Nous croyons en un seul Seigneur, Jésus-Christ,
le Fils unique de Dieu,
engendré du Père avant tous les siècles,
Lumière venue de la Lumière,
vrai Dieu venu du vrai Dieu,
engendré, non pas créé,
consubstantiel au Père;
par lui tout a été fait.
Pour nous et pour notre salut il descendit des cieux;
par le Saint-Esprit il a pris chair
de la Vierge Marie
et il s'est fait homme.
Il a été crucifié pour nous sous Ponce Pilate,
il a souffert, il a été enseveli,
il est ressuscité le troisième jour selon les Ecritures,
il est monté aux cieux.
Il siège à la droite du Père
et il reviendra dans la gloire
juger les vivants et les morts;
son règne n'aura pas de fin.

Nous croyons en l'Esprit Saint,
qui est Seigneur et donne la vie,
qui procède du Père,
qui avec le Père et le Fils
est adoré et glorifié,
qui a parlé par les Prophètes.
Nous croyons l'Eglise une, sainte, catholique et apostolique.
Nous confessons un seul baptême pour le pardon des péchés.
Nous attendons la résurrection des morts
et la vie du monde à venir. Amen.

36 *Glaubensbekenntnis von Nizäa — Konstantinopel* (Text von 381)

Wir glauben an den einen Gott,
den Vater, den Allmächtigen,
der alles geschaffen hat, Himmel und Erde,
die sichtbare und die unsichtbare Welt.

Wir glauben an den einen Herrn Jesus Christus,
Gottes eingeborenen Sohn,
aus dem Vater geboren vor aller Zeit,
Licht vom Licht,
wahrer Gott vom wahren Gott,
gezeugt, nicht geschaffen,
eines Wesens mit dem Vater;
durch ihn ist alles geschaffen.
Für uns Menschen und zu unserm Heil ist er von Himmel gekommen,
hat Fleisch angenommen durch den Heiligen Geist
von der Jungfrau Maria
und ist Mensch geworden.
Er wurde für uns gekreuzigt unter Pontius Pilatus,
hat gelitten und ist begraben worden,
ist am dritten Tage auferstanden nach der Schrift
und aufgefahren in den Himmel.
Er sitzt zur Rechten des Vaters
und wird wiederkommen in Herrlichkeit,
zu richten die Lebenden und die Toten;
seiner Herrschaft wird kein Ende sein.

Wir glauben an den Heiligen Geist,
der Herr ist und lebendig macht,
der aus dem Vater hervorgeht,
der mit dem Vater und dem Sohn
angebetet und verherrlicht wird,
der gesprochen hat durch die Propheten;
und die eine, heilige, katholische und apostolische Kirche.
Wir bekennen die eine Taufe zur Vergebung der Sünden.
Wir erwarten die Auferstehung der Toten
und das Leben der kommenden Welt. Amen.

36 *Símbolo de Nicea-Constantinopla* (texto de 381)

Creemos en un solo Dios,
Padre todopoderoso,
Creador de cielo y tierra,
de todo lo visible y lo invisible.

Creemos en un solo Señor, Jesucristo,
Hijo único de Dios,
nacido del Padre antes de todos los siglos:
Luz de Luz,
Dios verdadero de Dios verdadero,
engendrado, no creado,
de la misma naturaleza que el Padre,
por quien todo fue hecho;
que por nosostros y por nuestra salvación bajó del cielo,
y por obra del Espíritu Santo
se encarnó de María, la Virgen,
y se hizo hombre;
y por nuestra causa fue crucificado en tiempos de Poncio Pilato:
padeció y fue sepultado,
y resucitó al tercer día según las Escrituras,
y subió al cielo,
y está sentado a la derecha del Padre;
y de nuevo vendrá con gloria
para juzgar a vivos y muertos,
y su reino no tendrá fin.

Creemos en el Espíritu Santo,
Señor y dador de vida,
que procede del Padre,
que con el Padre y el Hijo
recibe una misma adoración y gloria,
y que habló por los profetas.
Creemos que la Iglesia es una, santa, católica y apostólica,
Reconocemos un solo bautismo para el perdón de los pecados.
Esperamos la resurrección de los muertos
y la vida del mundo futuro. Amén.

II

37 *Apostles' creed*

I believe in God,
  the Father almighty,
  Creator of heaven and earth.

I believe in Jesus Christ,
  his only Son, our Lord.
  He was conceived
  by the power of the Holy Spirit,
  and born of the Virgin Mary.

The Tree of Life, 17th century Byzantine icon • *L'arbre de vie, icône byzantine du 17e siècle* • Der Baum des Lebens, Byzantinische Ikone des 17. Jh. • *El árbol de la vida, icono bizantino del siglo XVII*

He suffered under Pontius Pilate,
was crucified, died,
and was buried.
He descended to the dead.
On the third day
he rose again.
He ascended into heaven,
and is seated
at the right hand of the Father.
He will come again
to judge the living and the dead.

I believe in the Holy Spirit,
the holy, catholic Church,
the communion of saints,
the forgiveness of sins,
the resurrection of the body,
and the life everlasting. Amen.

37   *Symbole des Apôtres*

Je crois en Dieu,
le Père tout-puissant,
Créateur du ciel et de la terre.

Je crois en Jésus-Christ,
son Fils unique,
notre Seigneur,
qui a été conçu du Saint-Esprit
et qui est né de la Vierge Marie;
il a souffert sous Ponce-Pilate,
il a été crucifié, il est mort,
il a été enseveli,
il est descendu au séjour des morts;
le troisième jour, il est ressuscité des morts;
il est monté aux cieux;
il siège à la droite de Dieu,
le Père tout-puissant,
d'où il viendra
juger les vivants et les morts.

Je crois en l'Esprit Saint,
la sainte Eglise catholique,
la communion des saints,

la rémission des péchés,
la résurrection de la chair
et la vie éternelle. Amen.

37 *Das Apostolische Glaubensbekenntnis*

Ich glaube an Gott,
den Vater, den Allmächtigen,
den Schöpfer des Himmels und der Erde.

Ich glaube an Jesus Christus,
seinen eingeborenen Sohn,
unsern Herrn,
empfangen durch den Heiligen Geist,
geboren von der Jungfrau Maria,
gelitten unter Pontius Pilatus,
gekreuzigt, gestorben
und begraben,
hinabgestiegen in das Reich des Todes,
am dritten Tage
auferstanden von den Toten,
aufgefahren in den Himmel;
er sitzt zur Rechten Gottes,
des allmächtigen Vaters;
von dort wird er kommen,
zu richten die Lebenden und die Toten.

Ich glaube an den Heiligen Geist,
die heilige christliche Kirche,
Gemeinschaft der Heiligen,
Vergebung der Sünden,
Auferstehung der Toten
und das ewige Leben. Amen.

Contemporary affirmations of faith

Affirmations contemporaines de la foi

Glaubensbekenntnisse der Gegenwart

Afirmaciones contemporáneas de fe

38

I believe in the living God,
the Parent of all humankind
who creates and sustains
the universe in power and in love.

I believe in Jesus Christ,
God incarnate on earth,
who showed us by his
        words and work,
        suffering with others,
        conquest of death,
what human life ought to be
and what God is like.

I believe that the Spirit of God
is present with us
now and always,
and can be experienced
in prayer, in forgiveness,
in the Word, the Sacraments,
the community of the Church
and all that we do.
Amen.

38

Ich glaube an den lebendigen Gott,
den Vater des ganzen Menschengeschlechts,
der das All in Macht und Liebe
geschaffen hat und erhält.

Ich glaube an Jesus Christus,
menschgewordener Gott auf Erden,
der uns gezeigt hat durch seine
    Worte und Taten,
    Leiden mit anderen,
    Überwindung des Todes,
was menschliches Leben sein sollte
und wie Gott ist.

Ich glaube, dass der Geist Gottes
bei uns gegenwärtig ist,
jetzt und immerdar,
und erfahren werden kann
in Gebet und Vergebung, in Wort und Sakrament,
in der Gemeinschaft der Kirche
und in allem, was wir tun.
Amen.

38

Creo en el Dios Vivo,
Padre de toda la humanidad,
que crea y mantiene el
universo con su poder y su amor.

Creo en Jesucristo,
Dios encarnado en la Tierra,
que nos enseñó con sus
    palabras y actos,
    su sufrimiento con los otros
    su triunfo sobre la Muerte
lo que debe ser la vida humana
y cómo es Dios.

Creo que el Espíritu de Dios
está presente con nosotros
ahora y siempre,
y que podemos experimentarlo
en la oración, en el perdón,
en la Palabra, los Sacramentos,
en la comunidad de la Iglesia
y en todo lo que hacemos.
Amén.

39

We are not alone; we live in God's world.

We believe in God
 who has created and is creating;
 who has come in Jesus, to reconcile
  and make new.

We trust God
 who calls us to be the church;
 to love and serve others;
 to seek justice and resist evil;
 to proclaim Jesus, crucified and risen,
  our judge and our hope.

In life, in death, in life beyond death,
 God is with us.
We are not alone.

Thanks be to God.

39

Wir sind nicht allein; wir leben in Gottes Welt.

Wir glauben an Gott,
 der die Welt geschaffen hat und in ihr wirksam ist,
 der in Jesus gekommen ist, um zu versöhnen und neu zu machen.

Wir vertrauen auf Gott,
 der uns beruft, Kirche zu sein;
 andere zu lieben und ihnen zu dienen;
 Gerechtigkeit zu suchen und Bösem zu widerstehen;
 Jesus zu verkünden, den Gekreuzigten und Auferstandenen,
  unseren Richter und unsere Hoffnung.

Im Leben, im Tod und im Leben nach dem Tod
 ist Gott mit uns.
Wir sind nicht allein.

Dank sei Gott.

39

Nous ne sommes pas seuls; nous vivons dans le monde de Dieu.

Nous croyons en Dieu
    qui a créé et crée toujours,
    qui est venu en Jésus, pour réconcilier et renouveler.

Nous avons foi en Dieu
    qui nous appelle à être l'Eglise,
    à aimer et à servir les autres,
    à rechercher la justice et à résister au mal,
    à proclamer Jésus crucifié et ressuscité,
        notre juge et notre espérance.

Dans la vie, dans la mort, dans la vie par-delà la mort,
    Dieu est avec nous.
Nous ne sommes pas seuls.

Rendons grâces à Dieu.

General prayers
Prières sans thème précis
Allgemeine Gebete
Oraciones varias

Opening prayers ● *Prières d'ouverture*
Eröffnungsgebete ● *Oraciones de apertura*

40

Lord, teach us the silence of humility
  the silence of wisdom
  the silence of love
  the silence that speaks without words
  the silence of faith
Lord, teach us to silence our own hearts and minds
  that we may listen to the movement of the Holy Spirit within us
  and feel your presence in the depth of our being. Amen.

40

Seigneur, enseigne-nous le silence et l'humilité
  le silence de la sagesse
  le silence de l'amour

The donkey is a symbol of humility and service ● *L'âne est symbole d'humilité et de service* ● Der Esel symbolisiert Bescheidenheit und Dienst ● *El asno es símbolo de humildad y servicio*

le silence qui parle sans paroles
le silence de la foi.
Seigneur, enseigne-nous le silence de nos cœurs et de nos esprits
pour que nous puissions écouter le mouvement du
Saint-Esprit en nous
et sentir ta présence au profond de notre personne.

40

Señor, enséñanos el silencio de humildad
el silencio de sabiduría
el silencio de amor
el silencio que habla sin palabras
el silencio de fe.
Señor, enséñanos a silenciar nuestros corazones y mentes
para que podamos escuchar el aleteo del Espíritu Santo en nosotros
y sentir tu presencia en el fondo de nuestro ser.

41

Gracious and Holy God,
Give us wisdom to perceive thee,
Diligence to seek thee,
Eyes to behold thee,
A heart to meditate upon thee,
And a life to proclaim thee
through Jesus Christ our Lord. Amen.

41

Dieu saint et miséricordieux,
donne-nous la sagesse pour te percevoir,
l'assiduité pour te chercher,
des yeux pour te contempler,
un cœur pour méditer sur toi,
et une vie pour te proclamer,
par Jésus-Christ, notre Seigneur. Amen.

41

Gnädiger und heiliger Gott,
Gib uns Weisheit, Dich zu erkennen;
Eifer, Dich zu suchen;
Augen, Dich zu erblicken;
ein Herz, über Dich nachzudenken;
Und ein Leben, Dich zu verkünden;
    Durch Jesus Christus, unseren Herrn. Amen.

42

God, who comes to us in our great joys, our crushing sorrows,
and in our life day-to-day, be with us now as we
share ourselves with one another in this time of......
In Jesus' name we pray. Amen.

42

Gott, der Du zu uns kommst in unserer grossen Freude, in unserem
grossen Schmerz und in dem dazwischenliegenden Alltagsleben, sei
mit uns jetzt, wo wir uns einander mitteilen in dieser Zeit des......
Darum bitten wir Dich in Jesu Namen. Amen.

42

Dios, que estás con nosotros en nuestras grandes alegrías, en nuestras
profundas penas y también en nuestra vida de todos los días, acompáñanos
ahora que estamos juntos en un compartir mutuo, en este tiempo de ......
Oremos en nombre de Cristo. Amén.

43

Loving God, whose glory outshines the sun, open our lives to
the inspiration of your Holy Spirit that we may more fully
reflect the glory of your love and share ourselves
with one another in this time of...
In Christ's name we pray. Amen.

96

43

Dieu d'amour, dont la gloire est plus resplendissante que le soleil,
ouvre nos vies à l'inspiration de ton Esprit Saint,
afin qu'elles reflètent plus fidèlement la gloire de ton amour
et soient l'image du partage en ce temps de...
Nous t'en prions au nom du Christ. Amen.

43

Dios de amor, cuya gloria brilla más que el sol, haz que
nuestras vidas reciban la inspiración de tu Espíritu Santo
para que podamos reflejar más plenamente la gloria de tu amor
y vivir en un compartir mutuo en este tiempo de...
Oremos en nombre de Cristo. Amén.

For understanding ● *Pour une meilleure compréhension des autres*
Für ein besseres gegenseitiges Verstehen ● *Para una mejor comprensión mutua*

44

Eternal God, whose image lies in the hearts of all people,
we live among peoples whose ways are different from ours,
    whose faiths are foreign to us,
    whose tongues are unintelligible to us.
Help us to remember that you love all people with your great love,
    that all religion is an attempt to respond to you,
    that the yearnings of other hearts are much like our own
    and are known to you.
Help us to recognize you in the words of truth, the things of beauty,
    the actions of love about us.
We pray through Christ, who is a stranger to no one land more than to
another, and to every land no less than to another.

44

Dieu éternel, dont l'image réside au cœur de chacun,
nous vivons parmi des gens dont les chemins diffèrent des nôtres,
    dont la foi nous est étrangère,
    dont la langue nous est incompréhensible.
Aide-nous à nous rappeler que tu aimes tous les êtres
    dans ton grand amour,
        que toute religion est une tentative pour te répondre,
        que les désirs du cœur des autres sont très semblables aux nôtres
        et sont connus de toi.
Aide-nous à te reconnaître dans les paroles vraies,
    les choses belles, les actions d'amour à notre égard.
Nous prions par le Christ qui n'est pas plus étranger dans un pays
que dans un autre, et pas moins dans tel pays que dans tel autre.

44

Ewiger Gott, dessen Bild im Herzen aller Menschen liegt.
Wir leben unter Völkern, die anders denken als wir,
    deren Glaubensweise uns fremd,
    deren Sprachen uns unverständlich sind.
Hilf uns, nie zu vergessen, dass du in deiner grossen Liebe
    alle Menschen liebst,
        dass jede Religion ein Versuch ist, dir zu antworten,
        dass die Sehnsucht anderer Herzen in vielem unserer gleicht
        und du sie kennst.
Hilf uns, dass wir in dir die Worte der Wahrheit erkennen,
    die Schönheit sehen,
        das Handeln der Liebe für uns spüren.
Wir bitten um Christi willen,
der keinem Land fremder ist als irgendeinem anderen,
und jedem Land nicht weniger fremd als irgend einem anderen.

45

Lord God, we come to adore you,
You are the ground of all that is.
You hold us in being, and without you we could not be.
Before we were born, before time began,
    before the universe came into being, you were;
When time is finished, when the universe is no more,
    you will still be.
Nothing can take your power from you.
And in your presence we can only be silent
    before the mystery of your being, for no words of ours can do
    justice to your glory.

        (silence)

45

Herr, unser Gott, wir kommen, dich anzubeten.
Du bist der Grund von allem, was lebt und besteht.
Du erhältst uns am Leben und ohne dich wären wir nicht da.
Ehe wir geboren waren, ehe die Zeit begann,
    ehe das All entstand, warst du da.
Wenn die Zeit endet und kein All mehr sein wird,
    wirst du noch immer da sein.
Niemand kann dir deine Macht rauben.
Und in deiner Gegenwart können wir still werden
    vor dem Geheimnis deines Wesens,
    denn kein einziges Wort, das wir sprechen,
    entspricht deiner Herrlichkeit.

        (Stille)

45

Señor Dios, venimos a adorarte.
Tú eres el principio de todas las cosas.

Tú nos mantienes en vida, sin ti no existiríamos.
Antes de que hubiéramos nacido, antes del comienzo del tiempo,
   antes de la existencia del universo, Tú ya existías.
Cuando el tiempo se acabe, cuando ya no exista el universo,
   Tú seguirás existiendo.
Nada ni nadie puede quitarte tu poder.
Y en tu presencia solo podemos guardar silencio ante
   el misterio de tu existencia, porque nuestras palabras
   no pueden rendir justicia a tu gloria.

   (silencio)

At the eucharist • *Pour l'eucharistie*
Beim Abendmahl • *En la eucaristía*

46

O Risen Christ, who made yourself known to the disciples
in the breaking of the bread at Emmaus;
the bread we break at this table
is a sign of the brokenness of all the world;
through our sharing in the Bread of Life
in our many Christian communions,
open our eyes and hands to the needs of all people.
Let our hearts burn to share your gifts
and help us to go forth with one another with Bread:
Bread of Hope, Bread of Life, Bread of Peace.

46

Christ ressuscité, tu t'es fait connaître à tes disciples
en rompant le pain à Emmaüs.
Le pain que nous rompons à cette table
est un signe des divisions du monde;
en nous faisant communier au pain de vie
dans nos diverses communions chrétiennes,
ouvre nos yeux et nos mains aux besoins de tous les êtres humains.

Allume en nos cœurs le désir de partager tes dons
et aide-nous à aller dans le monde avec ce pain,
pain d'espérance, pain de vie, pain de paix.

46

Oh Cristo Resucitado, que te diste a conocer a los discípulos
al partir el pan en Emaús;
el pan que partimos en esta mesa
es un signo de la división del mundo entero;
permite que al compatir el Pan de Vida
en nuestras diversas comuniones cristianas,
se abran nuestros ojos y manos
a las necesidades de todos los seres humanos.
Enciende en nuestros corazones el deseo
de compartir tus dones y ayúdanos a vivir juntos con ese Pan:
Pan de Esperanza, Pan de Vida, Pan de Paz.

Closing prayers ● *Prières de clôture*
Schlussgebete ● *Oraciones finales*

47

May the love of the Lord Jesus draw you to himself:
May the power of the Lord Jesus strengthen you in his service.
May the joy of the Lord Jesus fill your spirit
And the blessing of God Almighty, the Father, the Son and the
Holy Spirit, be upon you and remain with you for ever. Amen.

47

Que l'amour du Seigneur Jésus vous attire à lui.
Que la puissance du Seigneur Jésus vous fortifie à son service.
Que la joie du Seigneur Jésus emplisse vos esprits,
et que la bénédiction du Dieu tout-puissant, Père, Fils et Saint-Esprit
soit sur vous et reste avec vous pour toujours. Amen.

47

Möge die Liebe des Herrn Jesus Christus dich zu ihm hinziehen.
Möge die Kraft des Herrn Jesus Christus dich in seinem Dienst stärken.
Möge die Freude des Herrn Jesus deinen Geist erfüllen.
Und: Der Segen Gottes des Allmächtigen, des Vaters, des Sohnes
und des Heiligen Geistes, sei und bleibe mit dir für immer. Amen.

48

The blessing of the God of Sarah and of Abraham,
the blessing of the Son, born of Mary,
the blessing of the Holy Spirit who broods over us
    as a mother over her children,
be with you all. Amen.

48

Der Segen des Gottes von Sarah und Abraham,
der Segen des Sohnes, von Maria geboren,
der Segen des Heiligen Geistes, der über uns wacht
    wie eine Mutter über ihre Kinder,
sei mit euch allen. Amen.

48

La bendición del Dios de Sara y de Abraham,
La bendición del Hijo, nacido de María,
la bendición del Espíritu Santo que vela por nosotros
    como una madre por sus hijos,
descienda sobre todos ustedes. Amén.

49

As the earth keeps turning, hurtling through space,
and night falls and day breaks from land to land,
Let us remember people — waking, sleeping, being born, and dying —
one world, one humanity.
Let us go from here in peace. Amen.

49

Tandis que la terre tourne, lancée dans l'espace,
que tombe la nuit et s'ouvre le jour d'un pays à l'autre,
souvenons-nous des gens qui s'éveillent, qui dorment,
qui naissent et qui meurent, un seul monde, une seule humanité.
Allons en paix. Amen.

49

Da die Erde sich dreht, durchziehend den Raum,
da die Nacht hereinbricht und der Tag heraufdämmert
von Land zu Land, gedenken wir der Menschen,
die erwachen, schlafen, geboren werden und sterben,
— der einen Welt, der einen Menschheit.
Lasst uns gehen in Frieden. Amen.

49

Así como la tierra no cesa de girar, a través del espacio,
y las noches suceden a los días de unos países a otros
Recordemos a la humanidad — que camina, duerme, nace y muere — un
solo mundo, una sola humanidad.
Regresemos en paz. Amén.

50

Lead us from death to life,
        from falsehood to truth.
Lead us from despair to hope,
        from fear to trust.
Lead us from hate to love,
        from war to peace.
Let peace fill our heart, our world, our universe.

50

Conduis-nous de la mort à la vie,
        du mensonge à la vérité.

Conduis-nous du désespoir à l'espérance,
de la peur à la confiance.
Conduis-nous de la haine à l'amour,
de la guerre à la paix.
Que la paix remplisse notre cœur, notre monde, notre univers.

50

Führe uns vom Tod zum Leben,
von der Unwahrheit zur Wahrheit.
Führe uns von der Verzweiflung zur Hoffnung,
von der Angst zum Vertrauen.
Führe uns vom Hass zur Liebe,
vom Krieg zum Frieden.
Lass Frieden erfüllen unser Herz, unsere Welt, unser All.

50

Condúcenos de la muerte a la vida,
de la falsedad a la verdad.
Condúcenos de la desesperación a la esperanza,
del miedo a la confianza.
Condúcenos del odio al amor,
de la guerra a la paz.
Permite que la paz llene nuestros corazones, nuestro mundo,
nuestro universo.

Music
Musique
Musik
Música

Index of first lines
Répertoire des titres
Verzeichnis der Liedanfänge
Lista de títulos

Agios o Theos 15
Alabemos al Señor 24
Amen 38
Amin, haleluya! 21
And everyone 'neath the vine and fig tree 34
Aripamevi o Pachois 8
A ti, Señor, te pedimos 10
A toi le règne 18
Au cœur de notre vie 45
Auf, bringt Gaben und Lob herbei 53
Auf dem Sinaistein stand geschrieben 56
Ayant confondu les langues de l'univers 7
Bajo la higuera y el parral 34
Ba ni ngyeti Ba Yawe 24
Because he came into our world . 51
Behold, how pleasant 4
Bereitet den Weg des Herrn 20
Bless and keep us, Lord 61
Bo toi Israel 26
Ch'iu Chu lienmin women 12
Christ is risen from the dead . . . 29
Dans notre monde d'aujourd'hui . 1
Dein ist die Herrschaft 18
Dem Herren will ich folgen 47
Der Gott aller Menschen 60
Des riches sont devenus pauvres . 35
Do thou remember me 8
Edinstvo Tserkvi 55
Einheit für deine Kirche 55
Ein jeder braucht sein Brot, sein Wein 34
El cielo canta alegría 23
El espíritu de Dios está sobre mí . 25
En medio de la vida 45
Gloria al Señor 9
Hallelujah! 22
Haneul naneun sereul bora 50
Heaven is singing for joy 23
Herr, du bist überall! 28
Herr ist Jesus Christus 27

Het bôt ba to ba'a 2
Himmel erklingen vor Freude . . 23
Hosanna 33
Hristos a înviat din morţi 29
I am the way, the truth and the life 36
Ich will dich loben, Herr, mein Gott 59
In den Tälern, auf den Höhen . . 57
In the rock it was written on Sinai 56
In unser Leben, in unsere Geschichte 51
It's no life, no life at all 42
I will extol my God, my King . . 59
Jaya ho 58
Jesucristo, la vida del mundo . . . 40
Jesus Christ is Lord 27
Jesus Christ—the life of the world 40
Jésus-Christ, la vie du monde . . 40
Jesus Christus – das Leben der Welt 40
Jésus-Christ, vie du monde 44
Jesus Christ, whose passion claims us 62
Jésus est Seigneur 27
Jesus, Leben der Welt 43
Jesus, life of the world 43
Jesus, where can we find you . . . 1
Jesus, wo lässt du dich finden . . 1
Je t'exalterai, mon Dieu, mon roi 59
Kamponder'Omukama 47
Koi au na sala na dina na bula . . 36
Komm, Herr, segne uns 61
Kyrie eleison 11
Kyrie eleison 14
Lågorna är många 54
Lamb of God 31
Là où deux ou trois 2
Laudate omnes gentes 32
Let us praise the Lord our God . 24
Let us talents and tongues employ 53
Lord God, your love has called us here 48
Lord, have mercy on us 12
Lord, you are everywhere! 28
Many are the lightbeams 54
Maranatha, Alleluia 37

May our living be a feast	3	Sind zwei, sind drei	2
Mingled in all our living	45	Sobre estas tierras	49
Miren qué bueno	4	Strahlen brechen viele	54
Mitten in unsrem Leben	45	Teach me God to wonder	46
Muchos resplandores	54	Te exaltaré, mi Dios, mi Rey	59
Nao é vida a vida	42	Tenziwerumu komirai	30
Notre vie soit une fête	3	The God of us all	60
Oda ni oofe fee!	28	The Lord is my light	19
Oh behold the fowls of the air	50	The Spirit of the Lord is upon me	25
O Herr, mein Gott	13	Those who have been baptized in	
Oh praise the Lord	9	Christ	17
O Jesus Christ, life of the earth	39	Throughout this earth	49
O Lord, have mercy upon us	10	Through the byways and the high-	
O Lord, my God	13	ways	57
O Seigneur Dieu	13	Tuyo es el Reino	18
Osi is Christon evaptisthite	17	Über dem Schmerz	49
Par les chemins, plaines et monts	57	Unity of the Church	55
Pilgrims all are we	41	Unser Leben sei ein Fest	3
Plousioi eptohefsan kai epeinasan	35	Uyai!	5
Por los valles y los cerros	57	Vallesninta lomasninta	57
Porque El entró en el mundo	51	Veni Sancte Spiritus	6
Preisen lasst uns Gott, den Herrn	24	Ve Yashevu ish takhath gaphno	34
Rendons grâce au Seigneur	24	Voyageons ensemble	41
Seht die Vögel am Himmel euch an	50	Wer sind wir, die feiern, singen?	52
Seht doch, wie gut	4	Where two or three	2
Seigneur, enseigne-moi	46	Who are we who stand and sing?	52
Señor, mi Dios	13	Wir kommen, Herr, und wir bitten	10
Sfinte Dumnezeule	16	Ya, Tuhanku	13
Si dos o tres	2	Yours is the kingdom	18

* * *

Cantate Domino hymns related to the theme and sub-themes of the Assembly include the following • *Les cantiques suivants du Cantate Domino sont liés au thème et aux sous-thèmes de l'Assemblée* • Zu den Liedern aus Cantate Domino, die in Verbindung zum Thema und den Unterthemen der Vollversammlung stehen, gehören die folgenden • *Los himnos de Cantate Domino que se refieren al tema y a los subtemas de la Asamblea son los siguientes:*

Theme • *Thème* • Thema • *Tema*:
55, 63, 70, 71, 97, 99, 126, 131, 156, 161

Sub-theme I • *Sous-thème I* • Unterthema I • *Subtema I*:
1, 2, 3, 6, 7, 8, 10, 11, 12, 13, 15, 16, 17, 19, 20, 21, 22, 24, 28, 43, 47, 74, 108, 110, 111, 112, 113

Sub-theme II • *Sous-thème II* • Unterthema II • *Subtema II*:
2, 14, 29, 32, 33, 34, 35, 37, 38, 39, 40, 41, 49, 50, 53, 54, 55, 60, 66, 69, 77, 80, 84, 87, 88, 89, 91, 92, 93, 94, 95, 146, 172

Sub-theme III • *Sous-thème III* • Unterthema III • *Subtema III*:
22, 23, 26, 45, 46, 48, 59, 67, 79, 101, 105, 117, 131, 144, 147, 148, 149, 152

Sub-theme IV • *Sous-thème IV* • Unterthema IV • *Subtema IV*:
42, 99, 114, 118, 122, 123, 134, 135, 136, 137, 138, 139b, 140, 141, 143, 145, 151, 164

Doreen Potter   Doreen Potter, Jamaica

1. Je-sus, where can we find you in our world to - day? Je-sus, where can we find you In - car-nate Word to - day?

Refrain
Look at your bro-ther be - side you; look at your sis - ter be - side you. Look! Lis- ten! Care!

(Slower)

2. Jesus, in hand of the healer / can we feel you there? / Jesus, in word of the preacher / can we hear you there?

3. Jesus, in mind of the leader / can we know you there? / Jesus, in aims of the planner / can we find you there?

4. Jesus, in thought of the artist / can we sense you there? / Jesus, in work of the build-er / can we see you there?

5. Jesus, in face of the famished / can we see you there? / Jesus, in face of the prisoner / can we see you there?

6. Jesus, in faces of children / can we see you there? / Jesus, in all of creation / can we find you there?

1

Doreen Potter

Doreen Potter, Jamaica

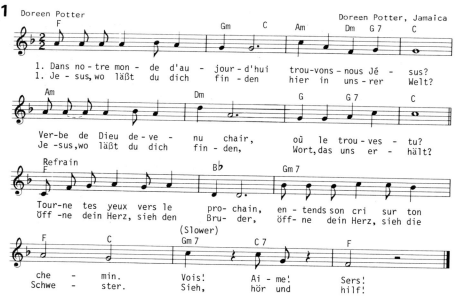

1. Dans no - tre mon - de d'au - jour-d'hui trou-vons - nous Jé - sus?
1. Je - sus, wo läßt du dich fin - den hier in uns - rer Welt?

Ver-be de Dieu de - ve - nu chair, où le trou - ves - tu?
Je -sus, wo läßt du dich fin - den, Wort, das uns er - hält?

Refrain

Tour-ne tes yeux vers le pro - chain, en - tends son cri sur ton
Öff - ne dein Herz, sieh den Bru - der, öff - ne dein Herz, sieh die

(Slower)

che - min. Vois! Ai - me! Sers!
Schwe - ster. Sieh, hör und hilf!

2. Dans le combat du médecin / voyons-nous Jésus? / Dans les mots du prédicateur, / le rencontres-tu?

3. Dans les calculs du chef d'état / sentons-nous Jésus? / Dans les verdicts des magistrats / le découvres-tu?

4. Peintre, musicien ou sculpteur, / connaît-il Jésus? / Dans l'oeuvre de l'entrepreneur / perçois-tu Jésus?

5. En secourant les affamés / voyons-nous Jésus? / En visitant les prisonniers / servons-nous Jésus?

6. Jésus, dans un regard d'enfant, / te saluons-nous? / Dans le monde entier en tourment, / te confessons-nous?

2. Jesus, in Händen des Arztes / spüren wir dich dort? / Jesus, in Worten gepredigt / hören wir dich dort?

3. Jesus, im Geist unsrer Mächt'gen / wissen wir dich dort? / Jesus, im Ziel unsrer Planer / finden wir dich dort?

4. Jesus, im Schaffen der Künstler / fühlen wir dich dort? / Jesus, im Werk der Erbauer / sehen wir dich dort?

5. Jesus, im hungrigen Nachbarn / sehen wir dich dort? / Jesus, im Blick der Gefang'nen / sehen wir dich dort?

6. Jesus, im Antlitz der Kinder / sehen wir dich dort? / Jesus, in all deiner Schöpfung / finden wir dich dort?

2

Matthew 18:20, arr.Bayiga Bayiga　　　　　　　　Bayiga Bayiga, Cameroon

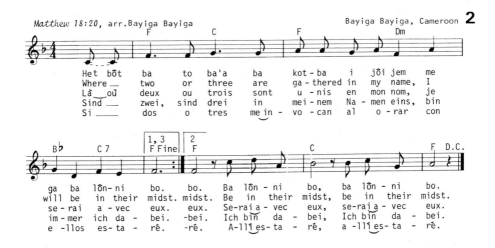

Het bōt ba to ba'a ba kot-ba i jōi jem me
Where two or three are ga-thered in my name, I
Lā oū deux ou trois sont u-nis en mon nom, je
Sind zwei, sind drei in mei-nem Na-men eins, bin
Si dos o tres me in-vo-can al o-rar con

ga ba lōn-ni bo. bo. Ba lōn-ni bo, ba lōn-ni bo.
will be in their midst. midst. Be in their midst, be in their midst.
se-rai a-vec eux. eux. Se-rai a-vec eux, se-rai a-vec eux.
im-mer ich da-bei. -bei. Ich bin da-bei, Ich bin da-bei.
e -llos es-ta-rē. -rē. A-llí es-ta-rē, a-llí es-ta-rē.

3

Josef Metternich team, Germany　　　　　　　　Peter Janssens, Germany

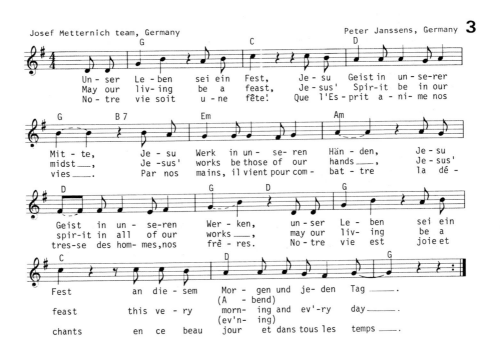

Un-ser Le-ben sei ein Fest, Je-su Geist in un-se-rer
May our liv-ing be a feast, Je-sus' Spir-it be in our
No-tre vie soit u-ne fête! Que l'Es-prit a-ni-me nos

Mit-te, Je-su Werk in un-se-ren Hän-den, Je-su
midst, Je-sus' works be those of our hands, Je-sus'
vies. Par nos mains, il vient pour com-bat-tre la dé-

Geist in un-se-ren Wer-ken, un-ser Le-ben sei ein
spir-it in all of our works, may our liv-ing be a
tres-se des hom-mes,nos frē-res. No-tre vie est joie et

Fest an die-sem Mor-gen und je-den Tag.
　　　　　　　　(A - bend)
feast this ve-ry morn-ing and ev'-ry day.
　　　　　　　　(ev'n- ing)
chants en ce beau jour et dans tous les temps.

Mi – ren qué bue – no, qué bue – no es. Mi – ren qué
Be – hold, how plea- sant, how good it is! Be – hold, how
Seht doch, wie gut und herr- lich es ist! Seht doch, wie

bue – no, qué bue – no es. 1. Mi – ren qué bue – no es
plea- sant, how good it is! 1. How plea - sant and har –
gut und herr - lich es ist! 1. Seht doch, wie gut und

cuan – do los her – ma – nos es – tán jun – tos:
mo –nious when God's peo – ple are to – ge – ther:
herr –lich ist's, wenn wir in Ein- tracht le – ben.

es co – mo a – cei – te bue – no de – rra – ma – do so - bre Aa - rón.
fra-grant as pre -cious oil when run- ning fresh on Aa - ron's beard.
Das ist, als wenn das Salb- öl glänzt auf Aa - rons schö- nem Haupt.

2. Miren qué bueno es cuando los hermanos están juntos: / se parece al rocío sobre los montes de Sión.

3. Miren qué bueno es cuando los hermanos están juntos, / porque el Señor ahí manda vida eterna y bendición.

2. How pleasant and harmonious when God's people are together: / refreshing as the dew upon the mountain of the Lord.

3. How pleasant and harmonious when God's people are together: / there the Lord God bestows his blessing - life for evermore.

2. Seht doch, wie gut und herrlich ist's, wenn wir in Eintracht leben. / Das ist erfrischend wie der Tau, der auf dem Zion fällt.

3. Seht doch, wie gut und herrlich ist's, wenn wir in Eintracht leben. / Dann segnet Gott und gibt uns Leben bis in Ewigkeit.

Patrick Matsikenyiri   Patrick Matsikenyiri, Zimbabwe **5**

Come, all you people, come to our Lord Jesus. Come, you mothers, you fathers! Jesus is calling us. He wants to go with us. We don't want our lives to perish until Jesus comes to lead us home. We are happy because we are free within the life of Jesus.

Venez, vous tous, venez vers notre Seigneur. Venez, vous mères, vous pères! Jésus nous appelle. Il veut cheminer avec nous. Nous ne voulons pas laisser périr nos vies jusqu'à ce que Jésus vienne nous ramener chez lui. Nous sommes heureux car nous sommes libres dans la vie de Jésus.

Kommt all ihr Völker, kommt zum Herrn Jesus. Kommt ihr Mütter, ihr Väter! Jesus ruft uns alle. Er will mit uns auf dem Weg sein. Wir wollen nicht aufgeben, bevor Jesus uns nach Hause bringt. Wir sind glücklich, denn Jesus macht uns frei.

Venid pueblos todos, venid a nuestro Señor Jesús. ¡Venid madres, padres! Jesús nos llama. El quiere ir con nosotros. No queremos que nuestras vidas perezcan antes que Jesús venga a llevarnos al hogar. Somos felices porque estamos libres dentro de la vida de Jesús.

6

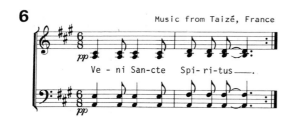

Music from Taizé, France

Ve - ni San-cte Spi - ri-tus———.

Come, Holy Spirit
Viens, Saint-Esprit
Komm, Heiliger Geist
Ven, Espíritu Santo

7

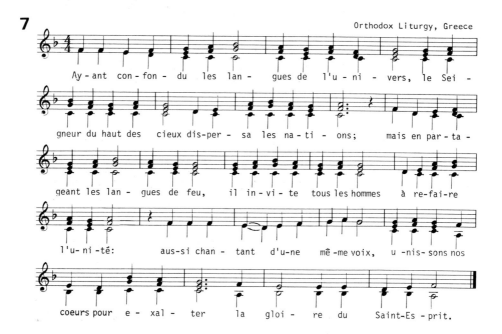

Orthodox Liturgy, Greece

Ay - ant con - fon - du les lan - gues de l'u - ni - vers, le Sei -
gneur du haut des cieux dis-per - sa les na - ti - ons; mais en par - ta -
geant les lan - gues de feu, il in - vi - te tous les hommes à re-fai-re
l'u - ni -té: aus-si chan - tant d'u-ne mê-me voix, u -nis-sons nos
coeurs pour e - xal - ter la gloi - re du Saint-Es - prit.

''Οτε καταβὰς τὰς γλώσσας συνέχεεν διεμέριζεν ἔθνη ὁ Κύριος. ''Οτε τοῦ πυρὸς τὰς γλώσσας διένειμεν εἰς ἑνότητα πάντας ἐκάλεσεν. Καὶ συμφώνως δοξάζομεν τὸ Πανάγιον Πνεῦμα.

When the Most High came down and confused the tongues he divided the nations, but when he distributed the tongues of fire he called all to unity; wherefore with one voice we glorify the Holy Spirit.

Al confundir las lenguas del universo el Señor del alto cielo dispersó las naciones; pero al distribuir las lenguas de fuego nos invita a todos a rehacer la unidad; por tanto, cantando a una voz, unamos nuestros corazones para exaltar la gloria del Espíritu Santo.

114

1. A - ri - pa - me - vi o Pa - chois: ak -
1. Do thou re - mem - ber me, O Lord, when

sha - ni khen tek - met - ou - ro .
thou wilt come in - to thy king - dom.

2. Aripamevi O Paouro: akshani khen tekmetouro.

3. Aripamevio Fi ethouab: akshani khen tekmetouro.

2. Do thou remember me, O King, when thou wilt come into thy kingdom.

3. Do thou remember me, Holy One, when thou wilt come into thy kingdom.

Traditional text   Bhajan melody, India **9**
Arr. I-to Loh

Oh praise the Lord. Oh praise the Lord. Oh praise the Lord, 1. God the
Glo - ri a al Se - ñor. Glo - ri a al Se - ñor. Glo - ri a al Se-ñor, 1. Dios, el

Fa - ther, fount of love. Oh praise the Lord. Oh praise the Lord _.
Pa - dre cre - a - dor. Glo - ri a al Se - ñor. Glo - ri a al Se -ñor _.

Oh praise the Lord, 1. God the Fa - ther, fount of love.
Glo - ri a al Se - ñor, 1. Dios, el Pa - dre cre - a - dor.

2. God the Son, our Saviour.   2. Dios, el Hijo, salvador.
3. God the Spirit, comforter.   3. Dios, Espíritu de amor.
4. God eternal Trinity.   4. Dios, eterna Trinidad.

1. Leader sings each phrase (marked by double bar-lines)
   and Congregation repeats after.
2. Begin slowly and gradually increase the dynamic and
   tempo from stz. 2. Slow down at stz. 4, and end slowly.
3. Form: ‖: AAB :‖ A
   4x

10 Ulises Torres, Chile   Chilean folk melody

1. A   ti, Se - ñor, te pe-di - mos per-dón en es-te mo-men - to
1. O   Lord, have mer-cy up-on us!   O   Lord have mer-cy up - on us!
1. Wir kom-men, Herr,und wir bit - ten: Gib jetzt uns dei-ne Ver-ge - bung!

por los pe-ca - dos de ac-cio-nes, pa - la-bras y   pen-sa-mien - tos.
For-give the wrong we are do-ing, our words and thoughts that of-fend you.
Ver-ge-bung für uns-re Ta - ten, für Wor-te und für Ge-dan - ken.

2. De tiempos inmemoriales / que nos hemos separado / de tu comunión bendita: / perdona nuestro pecado.

3. De tiempos inmemoriales / que nos hemos separado / de todos los demás hombres: / perdona nuestro pecado.

4. De tiempos inmemoriales, / en el alma del humano / hay luchas que lo destruyen: / perdona nuestro pecado.

2. As long as we can remember / we hide, O Lord, from your presence; / our hearts are yearning to know you. / O Lord, have mercy upon us!

3. How long, O Lord, have we wandered / alone in darkness, not loving / our sisters, brothers, your children. / O Lord, have mercy upon us!

4. As long as we can remember / our spirits are torn asunder / by greed and malice and hatred. / O Lord, have mercy upon us!

2. Wir haben in langen Zeiten / von dir uns, Herr, abgesondert, / von deiner guten Gemeinschaft. / Vergib die Schuld dieser Sünde!

3. Wir haben in langen Zeiten / von dir uns, Herr, abgesondert, / und damit auch von den Menschen. / Vergib die Schuld dieser Sünde!

4. Wir führen seit langen Zeiten / den Krieg in unserer Seele, / der Leben verneint und vernichtet. / Vergib die Schuld dieser Sünde!

Lord, have mercy on us.
Seigneur, aie pitié de nous.
Herr, erbarme dich unser.
Señor, ten piedad de nosotros.

11 Version I   Music from Taizé, France
                                                        Verse - Cantor

Ky - ri - e,   Ky - ri - e,   e - le - i - son.

Version II   I-to Loh, Taiwan **12**

求 主 憐 憫 我 們　求 基 督
Ch'iu— Chu lien - min— wo - men. Ch'iu— Chi - tu
Lord—, have mer - cy— on us. Christ —, have

憐 憫 我 們　求 主 憐 憫 我 們
lien - min— wo - men. Ch'iu— Chu lien - min— wo - men.
mer - cy— on us. Lord —, have mer - cy— on us.

Version III   Based on Javanese melody, Indonesia **13**
                                              Arr. Sutarno

Ya, Tu - han - ku,　ka - sih - a - ni - lah da - ku.
O Lord, my God,　have — mer - cy on me.
O Sei - gneur Dieu,　pi - tié pour ton ser - vi - teur.
O Herr, mein Gott,　er - barm dich ü - ber mich.
Se - ñor, mi Dios,　ten pie - dad — de — mí.

Ya, Tu - han - ku,　ka - sih - a - ni - lah da - ku.
O Lord, my God,　have — mer - cy on me.
O Sei - gneur Dieu,　pi - tié pour ton ser - vi - teur.
O Herr, mein Gott,　er - barm dich ü - ber mich.
Se - ñor, mi Dios,　ten pie - dad — de — mí.

Version IV   Orthodox liturgy, USSR **14**

Ky - ri - e e - lei - son,　Ky - ri - e e - lei - son,

Ky - ri - e e - le - i - son.

117

Holy God, Holy Mighty, Holy Immortal! Have mercy on us.
Dieu saint, saint et fort, saint et immortel, aie pitié de nous.
Heiliger Gott, heiliger Mächtiger, heiliger Unsterblicher, erbarme dich unser.
Santo Dios, Santo Poderoso, Santo Inmortal ¡Ten misericordia de nosotros!

Version I

Orthodox liturgy, USSR

15

A - gi - os o The - os, A - gi - os Is - chi - ros,

A - gi - os — A - tha - na - tos, E - le - i - son i - mas.

Version II

Orthodox liturgy, Roumania

16

Sfin - te Dum - ne - ze - u - le, Sfin - te ta - re,

Sfin - te făr' de moar - te, — mi - lu - e - şte - ne pre — noi.

118

Galatians 3:27

῎Ο -σοι εἰς Χρι - στὸν ἐ - βα-πτί - σθη -τε _____ Χρι-στὸν_ ἐ - νε-
O -si is Chri - ston e - va-pti - sthi-te _____ Chri- ston_ e - ne-
Those who have been bap - tized in Christ have put on Christ for

δύ-σα-σθε ἀλ-λη-λού - ι - α Δόξα Πατρὶ καὶ Υἱῷ καὶ ᾿Αγίῳ
thī-sa-sthe Al-li-lu - i - a. Thoxa Patri ke Io ke Agio
ev -er-more. Al-le-lu - i - a. Glory to the Father and to the Son

Πνεῦμα - τι-καὶ νῦν καὶ ἀεὶ καὶ εἰς τοὺς αἰῶνας τῶν αἰ -
Pnevma - ti-ke nin ke ai ke is tus eonas ton e - o-
and to the Holy Spir - it_ now and forever - more,

ώνων῾Α-μήν Χρι-στὸν ἐ - νε -δύ-σα-σθε ἀλ-λη-λού - ι - α
non A-min Chri-ston_ e - ne -thi-sa-sthe Al-li-lu - i - a.
A -men, have put on Christ for ev -er-more. Al-le-lu - i - a.

Vous tous, qui avez été baptisés en Christ, vous avez revêtu le Christ. Alléluia. Gloire au Père, au Fils et au Saint-Esprit, maintenant et toujours et dans les siècles des siècles. Amen.

Denn ihr alle, die ihr auf Christus getauft seid, habt Christus angezogen. Ehre sei dem Vater und dem Sohn und dem Heiligen Geist jetzt und immerdar und von Ewigkeit zu Ewigkeit. Amen.

Porque todos los que habéis sido bautizados en Cristo, de Cristo estáis revestidos. Aleluya. Gloria sea al Padre y al Hijo y al Espíritu Santo, ahora y siempre, por los siglos de los siglos. Amén.

Matthew 6:13b, arr. Pablo Sosa

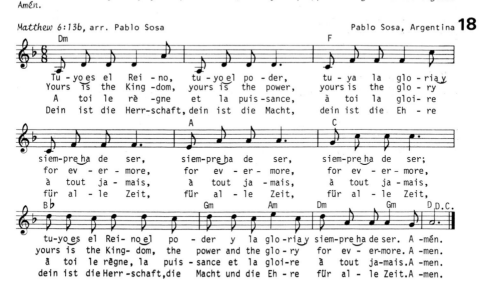

Tu - yo es el Rei - no, tu - yo el po - der, tu - ya la glo-ria y
Yours is the King -dom, yours is the power, yours is the glo - ry
A toi le rè -gne et la puis -sance, à toi la gloi - re
Dein ist die Herr-schaft, dein ist die Macht, dein ist die Eh - re

siem-pre ha de ser, siem-pre ha de ser, siem-pre ha de ser;
for ev - er - more, for ev - er- more, for ev - er - more,
à tout ja -mais, à tout ja -mais, à tout ja -mais,
für al - le Zeit, für al - le Zeit, für al - le Zeit,

tu-yo es el Rei - no el po - der y la glo-ria y siem-pre ha de ser. A -mén.
yours is the King- dom, the power and the glo - ry for ev - er-more. A -men.
à toi le règne, la puis - sance et la gloi-re à tout ja-mais. A -men.
dein ist die Herr-schaft, die Macht und die Eh - re für al - le Zeit. A -men.

19 *Psalm 27:1*   Music from Taizé, France

Theme I - Female voices

The Lord is my light, my light and sal-va-tion: in

him I trust, in him I trust. The

Theme II - Male voices

The Lord is my light, my

light and sal-va-tion: in him I trust, in him I trust. The

Le Seigneur est ma lumière et mon salut. En lui je me confie.
Der Herr ist mein Licht und mein Heil. Auf ihn vertraue ich.
El Señor es mi luz y mi salvación. En él confío.

Sing both themes simultaneously.

20 *Isaiah 40:3, arr. Volker Ochs*   Volker Ochs, Germany

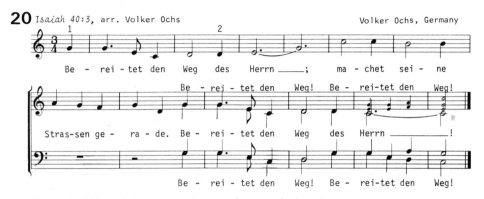

Be - rei - tet den Weg des Herrn _____; ma - chet sei - ne

Be - rei - tet den Weg! Be - rei-tet den Weg!

Stras-sen ge - ra - de. Be - rei - tet den Weg des Herrn _____!

Be - rei - tet den Weg! Be - rei-tet den Weg!

"Prepare the way of the Lord, make straight ... a highway."
"Préparez le chemin du Seigneur, aplanissez ... une route."
"Preparad camino al Señor; enderezad calzada ..."

21 Sutarno   Based on Javanese melody, Indonesia
                                                          arr. Sutarno

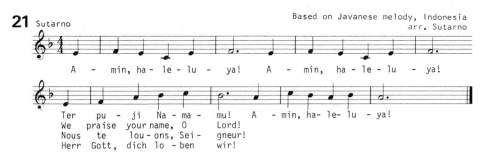

A - min, ha - le - lu - ya! A - min, ha - le - lu - ya!

Ter pu - ji Na - ma - mu! A - min, ha - le - lu - ya!
We   praise your name, O   Lord!
Nous te   lou - ons, Sei - gneur!
Herr Gott, dich lo - ben wir!

120

Hal-le-lu - jah ___, Hal-le-lu - jah, Hal-le-lu - jah ___, Hal-le-lu - jah!

Hal-le-lu - jah, Hal-le-lu, Hal-le-lu - jah, Hal-le-lu - jah!

Hal-le-lu - jah, Hal-le-lu - jah, Hal-le-lu - jah, Hal-le-lu - jah!

Pablo Sosa

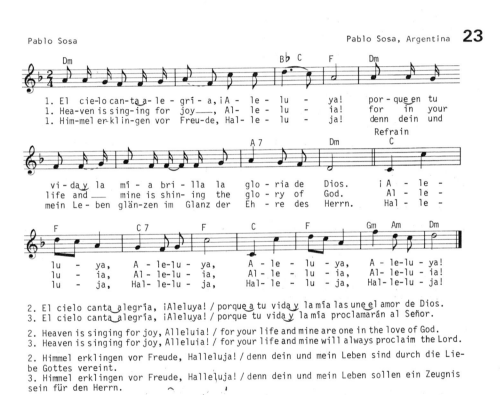

1. El cie-lo can-ta a-le - grí - a, ¡A - le - lu - ya! por - que en tu
1. Hea-ven is sing-ing for joy___, Al- le - lu - ia! for in your
1. Him-mel er-kl in-gen vor Freu-de, Hal- le - lu - ja! denn dein und

vi - da y la mí - a bri - lla la glo - ria de Dios. ¡A - le -
life and ___ mine is shin- ing the glo - ry of God. Al- le -
mein Le - ben glän-zen im Glanz der Eh - re des Herrn. Hal- le -

lu - ya, A - le-lu - ya, A - le - lu - ya, A - le-lu - ya!
lu - ia, Al- le-lu - ia, Al- le - lu - ia, Al- le-lu - ia!
lu - ja, Hal- le-lu - ja, Hal- le - lu - ja, Hal- le-lu - ja!

2. El cielo canta alegría, ¡Aleluya! / porque a tu vida y la mía las une el amor de Dios.
3. El cielo canta alegría, ¡Aleluya! / porque tu vida y la mía proclamarán al Señor.

2. Heaven is singing for joy, Alleluia! / for your life and mine are one in the love of God.
3. Heaven is singing for joy, Alleluia! / for your life and mine will always proclaim the Lord.

2. Himmel erklingen vor Freude, Halleluja! / denn dein und mein Leben sind durch die Liebe Gottes vereint.
3. Himmel erklingen vor Freude, Halleluja! / denn dein und mein Leben sollen ein Zeugnis
sein für den Herrn.

24

Cameroonian melody

Ba ni ngye - ti Ba Ya - we, ba ni ngye - ti Ba Ya - we,
Let us praise the Lord our God, let us praise the Lord our God,
Ren-dons grâ - ce au Sei-gneur, ren-dons grâ - ce au Sei-gneur,
Prei-sen laßt uns Gott, den Herrn, prei-sen laßt uns Gott, den Herrn,
A - la - be -mos al Se - ñor, a - la - be -mos al Se - ñor,

ba ni ngye - ti Ba Ya - we, A - men. Hal- le -lu-jah,
let us praise the Lord our God, A - men. Al - le-lu-ia,
ren-dons grâ - ce au Sei-gneur, A - men. Al - lé-lu-ia,
prei-sen laßt uns Gott, den Herrn, A - men. Hal- le-lu-ja,
a - la - be -mos al Se - ñor, A - mén. A - le-lu-ya,

Hal - le - lu - jah, Hal - le - lu - jah, A - men.
Al - le - lu - ia, Al - le - lu - ia, A - men.
Al - lé-lu - ia, Al - lé - lu - ia, A - men.
Hal - le - lu - ja, Hal - le - lu - ja, A - men.
A - le - lu - ya, A - le - lu - ya, A - mén.

25 *Luke 4:18-19, arr. Jim Strathdee*   Jim Strathdee, USA

The ___ spir-it of the Lord ___ is up - on me ___, be -
El Es - pí -ri - tu de Dios ___ es - tá so - bre mí por ___

cause he ___ has ___ a - noint - ed me ___ to ___ preach good ___ news to ___ the
cuan - to me ha con-sa-gra - do ___ pa-ra dar bue-nas nue-vas a los

poor ___. He has sent me to pro-claim re - lease to the cap - tives and re -
po -bres me ha man - da - do a pro - cla-mar ___ li-ber-tad ___ a los pre-sos ___ y la

cov-er-ing ___ of sight ___ to the blind ___, to set at lib-er - ty ___
vis - ta a los cie - gos ___ dar ___, po - ner en li-ber-tad ___

those who are op-press-ed ___, to pro-claim the ac-cept-a-ble year ___ of the Lord.
a los o - pri-mi -dos ___ pre-di-can-do el a - ño dig-no del Se - ñor.

Deuteronomy 6:4   Ghana **26**

Bo toi Is-rael Ye - ho - wa o nyon- mo le nyon-mo nyon-mo ko me ni.

1. Hal-le - lu - jah, Hal-le lu - jah, Hal-le lu - jah!
2. Ho -zi - a - na, ho -zi - a - na, ho -zi a - na!

ni.   Nyon-mo ko me ni, nyon-mo ko me ni.

Hear, O Israel: The Lord our God is one Lord.
Ecoute, Israël! Le Seigneur, notre Dieu, est le seul Seigneur.
Höre, Israel, der Herr, unser Gott, ist ein einiger Herr.
Oye, Israel: Jehová nuestro Dios, Jehová uno es.

Philippians 2:5-11, arr. Dieter Trautwein   Dieter Trautwein, Germany **27**

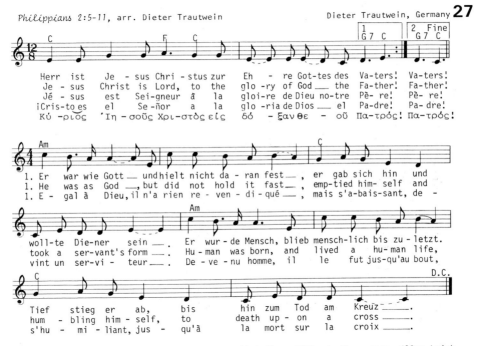

Herr ist Je - sus Chri - stus zur Eh - re Got-tes des Va-ters! Va-ters!
Je - sus Christ is Lord, to the glo - ry of God the Fa-ther! Fa-ther!
Jé - sus est Sei-gneur à la gloi-re de Dieu no-tre Pè- re! Pè- re!
¡Cris-to es el Se -ñor a la glo-ria de Dios el Pa-dre! Pa-dre!
Κύ -ριος Ἰη -σοῦς Χρι-στὸς εἰς δό - ξαν θε - οῦ Πα-τρός! Πα-τρός!

1. Er war wie Gott und hielt nicht da - ran fest , er gab sich hin und
1. He was as God ,but did not hold it fast , emp-tied him- self and
1. E - gal à Dieu,il n'a rien re - ven - di-qué ; mais s'a-bais-sant, de -

woll-te Die-ner sein . Er wur - de Mensch, blieb mensch-lich bis zu - letzt.
took a ser-vant's form . Hu-man was born, and lived a hu-man life,
vint un ser-vi - teur . De - ve -nu homme, il le fut jus-qu'au bout,

Tief stieg er ab, bis hin zum Tod am Kreuz .
hum - bling him - self, to death up - on a cross .
s'hu - mi - liant, jus - qu'à la mort sur la croix .

2. Drum gab ihm Gott den allerhöchsten Namen / hat ihn erhöht, damit um Jesu willen / sich jeder Mensch tief beugt und klar bekennt / vor aller Welt je in der eignen Sprache!

2. Therefore has God exalted him on high, / giv'n him the name that is above all names, / that at the name of Jesus all should bow, / and ev'ry tongue in heav'n and earth confess:

2. C'est pourquoi Dieu lui donne un nom glorieux, / pour qu'en son nom, sur terre, tous l'adorent / et d'un seul coeur le proclament Seigneur / sur notre terre comme dans les cieux!

28

1. O - da ni oo - fe fee! Nun - tsho o - da ni oo - fe fee! -fee!
1. Lord, you are ev' - ry - where! Lord God, you are ev' - ry - where! -where!
1. Herr, du bist ü - ber - all! Ü - ber - all bist du der Herr! Herr!

Na - mo po wo - ke le baa - tô o - he. O - da ni oo - fe fee! fee!
No one can ev - er be com - pared with you. Yes, you are ev' - ry - where! - where!
Niemand kann sich mit dir ver - glei - chen. Herr, du bist ü - ber - all! -all!

2. Oda ni oohe wa! Nuntsho oda ni oohe wa! / Namo po woke le baatô ohe. Oda ni oohe wa!

2. Lord, you are powerful! Lord God, you are powerful! / No one can ever be compared with you. Yes, you are powerful!

2. Herr, du hast große Kraft! Keiner ist so stark wie du! / Niemand kann sich mit dir vergleichen. Herr, du hast große Kraft!

29

Hris - tos a în - vi - at din morți, cu moar - tea pre moar - te căl -
Christ is ri - sen from the dead, tram - pling down Death by

cînd și ce - lor din mor - min - te vi -
death, and up - on those in the tomb be -

a - ță dă - ru - in - du - le!
stow - ing life, e - ter - nal life.

30

Ten - zi - we - ru - mu ko - mi - rai ne - su - zvi - no,

ku - ti - gu - wa - i no - ti - e - ri - swe - ndi - mwi.

Christ of the resurrection, stand by us now, so that at this moment we are made holy by you.

124

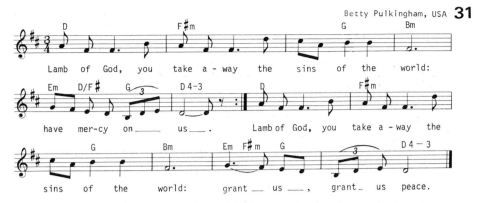

Lamb of God, you take a-way the sins of the world: have mer-cy on_ us_. Lamb of God, you take a-way the sins of the world: grant _ us _, grant_ us peace.

Agneau de Dieu, qui ôtes les péchés du monde, aie pitié de nous. Donne-nous ta paix.
Christe, du Lamm Gottes, der du trägst die Sünd' der Welt, erbarme dich unser. Gib uns
deinen Frieden.
Oh Cristo, cordero de Dios, que quitas el pecado del mundo, ten piedad de nosotros. Da-
nos tu paz.

Lau-da-te om-nes gen-tes, lau-da-te Do-mi-num. Lau-da-te om-nes gen-tes, lau-da-te Do-mi-num!

All peoples, praise the Lord!
Louez le Seigneur, tous les peuples!
Lobet alle Völker, lobet den Herrn!
¡Pueblos todos alabad al Señor!

Ho - san - na, ho - san - na, ho - san - na in ex - cel - sis.

34 Micah 4:3-4   Hebrew folk melody

Ve ya-she-vu ish_ ta-khath gaph-no ve ta-khath
And ev'-ry-one 'neath the vine and fig tree shall live in
Ein je-der braucht sein_ Brot, sein Wein_ und Frie-den
Ba-jo la hi-gue-ra y el pa-rral_ se sen-ta-
ya na-die la a-me-dren-ta-rá_ por-que el Se-

t'e-na-tho veeyn ma-kha-rid. rid.
peace and_ un-a-fraid. fraid.
oh-ne Furcht soll_ sein. sein.
rá la gen-te en paz;
ñor la am-pa-ra-rá.

Lo yis-u goi el-goi_ khe-rev_,
Plow-shares beat out of_ swords_ and guns_;
Pflug-scha-ren schmelzt aus Ge-weh-ren und Ka-no-nen,
Mar-ti-lla-rán sus es-pa-das y ca-ño-nes
no se al-za-rá gen-te con-tra_ gen-te

ve lo yil-me-dun od mil-kha-mah_! mil-kha-mah_!
and we will stud-y_ war no more_! war no more_!
daß wir in Frie-den bei-sam-men woh-nen! -sam-men woh-nen!
y las ha-rán ho-ces ya-za-do-nes;
ni en-sa-ya-rán pa-ra ir al fren-te.

וְיָשְׁבוּ אִישׁ תַּחַת גַּפְנוֹ / וְתַחַת תְּאֵנָתוֹ / וְאֵין מַחֲרִיד יֽ׃

לֹא יִשְׂאוּ גוֹי אֶל־גּוֹי חֶרֶב / וְלֹא־יִלְמְדוּן עוֹד מִלְחָמָה

35 Psalm 34:10 (adapt.)   Orthodox liturgy, Greece

Πλού-σι-οι ἐπ-τώ-χευ-σαν καὶ ἐ-πεί-να-σαν. Οἱ δὲ ἐκ-ζη-

τοῦν-τες τὸν Κύ-ρι-ον οὐκ ἐλ-λα-τω-θή-σον-ται παν-τὸς ἀ-γα-θοῦ.
Des ri-ches sont de-ve-nus pauv-res et ont con-nu la faim, mais ceux qui re-
cher-chent le Sei-gneur ne se-ront ja-mais pri-vés d'au-cun de ses bien-faits.

The rich have become poor and hunger; but those who seek the Lord lack no good thing.
Reiche sind arm geworden und haben Hunger; wer aber den Herrn sucht, braucht kein Gut zu entbehren.
Los ricos se han vuelto pobres y tienen hambre; pero los que buscan al Señor no tendrán falta de ningún bien.

1. Koi au na sa-la na di-na na bu-la, ka-ya ko Ji-
1. I am the way,— the truth and the life,— that's what Je-sus

su. Koi au na -su. Se-ga na sa-la e-da na
said. I am the said. With-out the way there is— no

se-se, se-ga na di-na e-da na we-le, se-ga na
go-ing, with-out the truth there is— no know-ing, with-out the

bu-la e-da na ru-sa. Koi au na sa-la na di-na na
life there is— no liv-ing. I am the way,— the truth and the

bu-la, ka-yo ko Ji-su. Koi au na -su.
life,— that's what Je-sus said. I am the said.

37 Music from Taizé, France

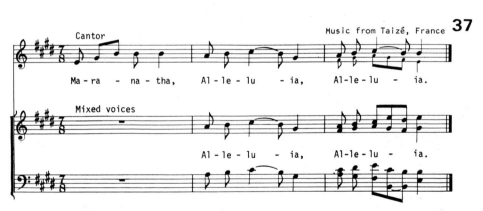

Cantor

Ma-ra-na-tha, Al-le-lu-ia, Al-le-lu-ia.

Mixed voices

Al-le-lu-ia, Al-le-lu-ia.

38 Hansruedi Willisegger, Switzerland

1. 2.
A - men. A - men. A - men. A - men.

127

39 Jane Parker Huber, USA

Trente quatre pseaumes de David, Geneva, 1551

1. O Je - sus Christ, life of the earth and light to
ev' - ry na - tion, breathe mean-ing in - to death
and birth, your Spir - it, our sal - va - tion.
Your per - fect life in ev' - ry age im - print a - fresh on
his -tory's page - life of the world, and our life!

2. O Jesus Christ, in whom we find / abundant life and caring, / grant us an open heart and mind, / each other's burdens bearing. / From others may we truly learn / what each can offer, turn by turn -/ life of the world, and our life!

3. O Jesus Christ, call us anew / to lives of firm decision. / Give youth and age your work to do / with courage, faith and vision. / Let justice be the measuring rod / of our devotion to our God -/ life of the world, and our life!

4. O Jesus Christ, best gift of God, / born, dead, and raised to save us, / friend of the pilgrim-way we've trod, / let nothing ill enslave us. / In unity life overflows / with richness God's good grace bestows -/ life of the world, and our life!

128

Dieter Trautwein, Germany   Herbert Beuerle, Germany **40**

Refrain   F   Gm   C

Je - sus   Chri - stus - das   Le - ben der   Welt   !   Je - sus
Je - sus   Christ ___ - the   life   of   the   world   !   Je - sus
Je - sus -   Christ ___,   la   vie _____   du   mon - de!   Je - sus -
¡Je - su -   cris - to,   la   vi - da del   mun - do!   ¡Je - su -

Dm   Gm   C   F   Fine   F

Chri - stus - das   Le - ben der   Welt ___!   1. Wer   le - ben   will, muß
Christ ___ - the   life of the   world ___!   1. To   live   is   to be
Christ ___,   la   vie _____ du   mon - de!   1. Si   tu   veux   vrai - ment
cris - to,   la   vi - da del   mun - do!   1. Vi - vir   es   el   a -

Bb   Dm   Gm   C   F

at - men mit   See - le, Leib und   Geist, die   Ga - ben   zu   emp -
o - pen in   bo - dy, soul and   mind, re - ceive what Christ has
vi - vre, re -   çois les dons de   Dieu, sa   grâ - ce   qui   dé -
lien - to que a -   ni - ma to - do   ser al   re - ci - bir los

Bb   Gm   C   F   D.C.

fan - gen,   die   Chri - stus uns ver - heißt.
pro - mised - God's   breath for hu - man - kind.
li - vre,   sa   paix qui vient des   cieux.
do - nes de   Cris - to y su po - der.

2. Wer leben will, muß leiden an allem, was zerstört, / durch Christus überwinden, was noch dem Tod gehört.

3. Wer leben will, muß wachsen, bis Gottes ganzes Reich / in Fülle sich entfaltet, verschieden und doch gleich.

4. Wer leben will, muß eins sein mit allen, die Gott liebt, / und Schranken niederbrechen, wo Christus Zeichen gibt.

2. To live is to be ready to fight the friends of death, / and rise with Christ the victor, to once again take breath.

3. To live is to grow daily in ways that lead to life, / God's kingdom, one, yet varied, encompassing all strife.

4. To live is to be one with all those whom God does love, / to break down ev'ry barrier to let Christ's Spirit move.

2. Si tu veux vraiment vivre, il te faudra souffrir, / il te faudra le suivre jusqu'à être martyr.

3. Si tu veux vraiment vivre, tu dois croître en amour / pour que son règne arrive et transforme nos jours.

4. Vivre, c'est l'espérance d'être un jour tous unis, / puisqu'en l'amour du Père, nous sommes unis en Christ.

2. Vivir es sufrimiento al enfrentar el mal, / y triunfo en Jesucristo, la muerte al derrotar.

3. Vivir es crecimiento, deseos de lograr / que el Reino se establezca, variado pero igual.

4. Vivir es esperanza y anhelo de unidad / con todos los que aman de Dios la voluntad.

41 R. Burn Purdon   R. Burn Purdon, Canada

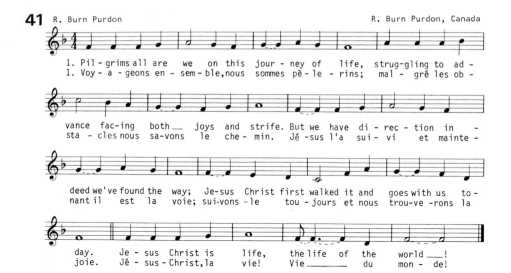

1. Pil - grims all are we on this jour - ney of life, strug-gling to ad-
1. Voy - a - geons en - sem - ble, nous sommes pè - le - rins; mal - gré les ob -

vance fac-ing both__ joys and strife. But we have di - rec - tion in -
sta - cles nous sa-vons le che - min. Jé -sus l'a sui - vi et mainte -

deed we've found the way; Je-sus Christ first walked it and goes with us to-
nant il est la voie; sui-vons -le tou - jours et nous trou-ve -rons la

day. Je - sus Christ is life, the life of the world __!
joie. Jé - sus - Christ, la vie! Vie_____ du mon - de!

2. We all need refreshment, renewal, rebirth; / lest we all should die like a plant with no earth. / But just like the plant, given water, earth and sun, / we all through Christ's Spirit have new life everyone. / Jesus Christ is life, the life of the world!

3. It takes many stones a strong structure to build; / each one is important so weak spots are filled. / We are living stones in God's temple on earth; / Jesus Christ the chief cornerstone of great worth. / Jesus Christ is life, the life of the world!

4. Many unknown riches lie hidden in the ground; / there is always joy when new treasure is found. / Likewise is the kingdom a find of great worth; / to possess its richness brings both joy and mirth. / Jesus Christ is life, the life of the world!

5. Many grains of wheat into flour must be ground, / if there's to be bread with enough to go 'round. / We are grains of wheat, Jesus Christ the true bread; / and through us, Christ's body, a hung'ring world is fed. / Jesus Christ is life, the life of the world!

6. An heir to a throne does in time wear a crown, / symbol of position, of power, of renown. / We are all joint heirs who with Christ do receive / each a crown of life, for in Christ we do believe. / Jesus-Christ is life, the life of the world!

2. Jésus dit qu'il faut que nous naissions de nouveau-/ une renaissance de l'Esprit et de l'eau. / Soyons comme un arbre à côté de l'eau planté; / Jésus est la source assurant notre santé. / Jésus-Christ, la vie! Vie du monde!

3. Pour construire un temple on emploie beaucoup de pierres; / chacune importante oui, chacune est nécessaire. / Nous sommes tous pierres vivantes et choisies, / et la pierre d'angle du temple est Jésus-Christ. / Jésus-Christ la vie! Vie du monde!

4. Il y a des richesses dans le sol enterrées; / joyeux est celui qui un trésor a trouvé. / Comme un tel trésor est le royaume de Dieu; / le trouver c'est vivre en Christ qui nous rend heureux. / Jésus-Christ, la vie! Vie du monde!

5. La farine est faite en moulant des grains de blé, / ainsi on peut faire un bon pain pour partager. / Nous sommes les grains, Jésus-Christ le pain vie. / L'Eglise est son corps ainsi le monde est nourri. / Jésus-Christ, la vie! Vie du monde!

6. La couronne est symbole de la renommée./ L'héritier d'un royaume pourra la porter. / Avec Jésus-Christ nous sommes tous héritiers. / La couronne de vie à nous sera donnée./ Jésus-Christ, la vie! Vie du monde!

1. Não é vi-da a vida que se vi-ve por en-ga-no,
1. It's no life, no life at all, that's root-ed in de-cep-tion,

es-sa tris-te vi-da que não tem ca-lor hu-ma-no.
it's no life when hu-man warmth is miss-ing from per-cep-tion.

Pois vi-ver a vi-da é mui-to mais do que a a-pa-rên-cia.
Liv-ing is a whole lot more than scram-bling for sur-vi-val,

de vi-ver a vi-da que só é so-bre-vi-vên-cia.
go-ing through the mo-tions with your neigh-bour as a ri-val.

Refrain

Je-sus Cris-to é a vi-da, é a vi-da do mun-do.
Je-sus Christ, he is the life, he is the life of the world___.

2. Não é vida a vida que se vive como escravo / sem ter voz ou vez, sem lar, abrigo nem centavo. / Pois viver a vida é como a busca da aventura: / só é vida a vida enquanto a liberdade dura.

3. Não é vida a vida que se vive sem futuro, / que só tem memória, só passado vago e escuro. / Pois viver a vida é muito mais do que a lembrança: / só é vida a vida que ressurge da esperança.

4. Essa vida é a vida que em Jesus nós alcançamos / quando junto a ele o mundo injusto transformamos, / e vencendo a morte, as opressões e a tirania, / viveremos sempre no seu Reino de alegria.

2. It's no life, no life at all, in slavery to suffer, / with no shelter or a voice or money for a buffer. / Living ought to be more like a wonderful adventure, / with the freedom to move out in any kind of venture.

3. It's no life, no life at all, when there's no future showing, / memory is not enough to keep a person going. / Living cannot be reliving of the past, discouraged, / life must be attainable and real for hope to flourish.

4. It is life, authentic life, that Jesus has to offer, / working with us to transform our world where people suffer. / Tyranny shall be no more and all oppression vanish; / in his kingdom full of joy the fear of death is banished.

Sister Lauretta Mather, USA

Je - sus ___, life of the world ___, change us in - to your bread
Je - sus ___, Le - ben der Welt ___, wand - le uns in das Brot,

___ bro - ken and shared ___. Je - sus ___, life of the world
___ das du ver - teilst ___. Je - sus ___, Le - ben der Welt

___, we are your bod- y ___, Je - sus Lord ___.
___, wir sind dein Leib ___, du un - ser Herr ___!

1. Our world is di - vi - ded and our church- es ___ are not one ___. Our
1. Die Welt ist zer - spal - ten, schon lang sind Kir - chen ent - zweit ___. Ge -

life as com - mu - ni - ty ___ has scarce - ly yet be - gun ___. But
mein - schaft nach dei - nem Geist bleibt aus, rückt fern und weit ___. Doch

you prayed for u - ni - ty ___, taught us that it would be ___ your
Ein - heit hast du er - fleht ___, dein Zei - chen, das die Welt ver -

sign ___. ___ we are your bod - y ___, Je - sus, Lord.
steht ___! ___ wir sind dein Leib ___, du un - ser Herr!

2. Around us is brokenness in nations and in homes. / We turn from each other and we struggle all alone. /But you draw all people near/ if we will only hear your word.

3. Survival is threatened but our refuge is in might. / We build up our weapons and then spend our lives in fright. /But you showed us how to live,/told us that we must give your peace.

4. The struggle for justice is so needed in our times. / Equality of persons has its limits and its lines./But you died to set us free,/ gave all humanity your life.

2. Das Leben zerbricht uns / in Volk, Familie und Haus. / Wir kehr'n uns den Rücken zu / und fechten's einsam aus. / Doch du bringst einander nah, / hören wir auf dein Wort, dein Ja!

3. Bedroht ist das Leben, / wer zu dir flieht, der hält stand. / Wenn wir uns mit Waffen droh'n, / stellt Angst uns an die Wand. / Doch Leben schenkst du, das lohnt, / Frieden, der gibt und sich nicht schont.

4. Den Kampf gegen Unrecht / hat sie nötig, unsre Welt. / Ums gleiche Recht für alle / ist traurig es bestellt. / Doch dein Tod will uns befrei'n, / Menschen nach deinem Bild zu sein.

New Caledonia **44**

1. Jé - sus - Christ, vie du monde, oui —, pa - role —— de l'E - van - gile.
Jé - sus - Christ, vie du monde, oui —, lu - mière —— de l'E - van - gile.

Refrain
1.-4. Ho - san - na, Ho - san - na, Ho - san - na, Al - lé - lu - ia —!

5. Tu as for - ti - fié mon âme, Je —— cé - lè - bre ton nom su - prême.
Reste au - près —— de mes blames pour —— con - quê - rir —— Jé - ru - sa - lem.

Refrain
5. Al - lé - lu - ia, Al - lé - lu - ia, Al - lé - lu - ia, A - men! Ho - san - na, Ho - san - na, Ho - san - na, Al - lé - lu - ia —!

2. Jésus-Christ, vie du monde, / oh pourquoi tant d'injustice. / Jésus-Christ, vie du monde, / oui, pour moi il est justice.

3. Jésus-Christ, vie du monde, / joie, paix et humilité. / Jésus-Christ, vie du monde, / justice et vérité.

4. Jésus-Christ, vie du monde, / obéissance, persévérance. / Jésus-Christ, vie du monde, / triomphe par l'espérance.

45 Mortimer Arias, Bolivia　　　　　　　　　　　　Antonio Auza, Bolivia

1. En me - dio de la vi - da es - tás pre - sen - te, oh Dios,
1. Min-gled in all our liv- ing your pre-sence, Lord, I feel,
1. Au coeur de no - tre vi - e, tu es pré - sent, Sei - gneur
1. Mit-ten in uns- rem Le - ben bist du, Gott, Ge - gen - wart:

más cer - ca que mí a - lien - to, sus- ten - to de mi ser.
clos-er than my own sigh - ing, your love sus-tain - ing me.
com - me l'air qu'on res - pi - re, le pain de no - tre corps,
birgst dich im A - tem - ho - len und als des Le - bens Puls

Tú im- pul - sas en mis ve - nas mi san - gre al pal - pi - tar
You cause the pulse of blood, Lord, to flow in ev' - ry vein,
le sang de nos ar - tè - res qui ryth - me no - tre coeur,
strömst du durch al - le A - dern, legst dei - nen Geist auf uns,

y el rit - mo de la vi - da vas dan-do al co - ra - zón.
my heart re-sponds in glad - ness, life's rhythm beats with - in.
les beau - tés de la ter - re qui en font la sa - veur.
bringst Schwung in uns - re Schrit - te, kommst Her - zen auf den Grund.

Refrain

Oh Dios de cie - lo y tie - rra, te sir - vo des - de a - quí;
O Lord of earth and heav - en, I give my life to you,
Dieu, au ciel et sur ter - re, je suis ton ser - vi - teur,
Gott Him - mels und der Er - de, dem un - ser Dienst ge - fällt,

te a - mo en mis her - ma - nos, te a - do - ro en la crea - ción ___.
lov - ing you in my neigh-bour, prais-ing you in the world ___.
je t'ai - me dans mes frè - res, toi, no - tre Cré - a - teur ___.
Lie - be zu dir braucht Men-schen, Lob-preis er - hält die Welt ___.

2. Tú estás en el trabajo / del campo o la ciudad. / Y es himno de la vida / el diario trajinar. / El golpe del martillo, / la tecla al escribir, / entonan su alabanza / al Dios de la creación.

3. Tú estás en la alegría / y estás en el dolor, / compartes con los hombres / la lucha por el bien. / En Cristo tú has venido / la vida a redimir, / y en prenda de tu reino / el mundo a convertir.

2. You stand beside the worker / in factory and farm; / daily incessant clamour / sounding a hymn of life. / In ev'ry hammer's pounding, / typewriter's clacking key, / we hear a tune of praising, / creation's melody.

134

3. You're in the sound of laughter / and in the flow of tears, / sharing with all your
people / the fight for human good. / You came in Christ incarnate / that life might be
redeemed,/pledging us to your kingdom,/helping the world to change.

2. Dans la peine des hommes, / en ville comme aux champs, / tu connais leur souffrance/
et souffres avec eux. / Le bruit de leurs machines / et les coups de marteau / font comme
un long cantique / qui monte jusqu'aux cieux.

3. Près de nous, dans nos joies / et dans notre douleur, / tu partages nos vies/et nous
offres ta paix. / En Christ, tu nous libères / pour être les témoins / jusqu'au bout de
la terre, / de ton règne qui vient.

2. Du bist in aller Arbeit / nahe in Land und Stadt, / bist Stimme der Gedrückten / im
täglichen Betrieb. / Wenn die Maschinen stampfen, / wenn eine Hand sich regt, / klingt
auf in vielen Weisen / Lob dir, du Schöpfer Gott.

3. Du bist in großer Freude, / du bist in tiefem Schmerz / einer, der uns begleitet, /
mitkämpft fürs Menschenwohl. / Du kommst und hast in Christus /Leben uns neu geschenkt,/
du zählst uns zu den Deinen, / änderst die alte Welt.

Walter Farquarson, Canada   Ron Klusmeier, Canada **46**

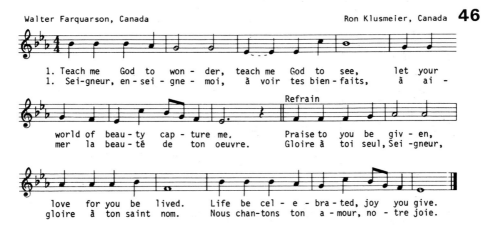

1. Teach me God to won - der, teach me God to see,   let your
1. Sei-gneur, en-sei - gne - moi, à voir tes bien-faits,   à ai -

world of beau-ty cap - ture me.   Praise to you be giv - en,
mer la beau-té de ton oeuvre.   Gloire à toi seul, Sei -gneur,

love for you be lived.   Life be cel - e - bra-ted, joy you give.
gloire à ton saint nom.   Nous chan-tons ton a -mour, no - tre joie.

2. Let me God be open, let me loving be, / let your world of people speak to me.

3. Let me God be ready, let me be awake, / in your present kingdom my place take.

4. Teach me God to know you, hear you when you speak, / see you in my neighbour when we
meet.

2. Dans mon coeur, mets l'amour, né de ton Esprit, / pour tous ceux qu'ici-bas, tu as
aimés.

3. Fais de moi l'instrument de ta sainte paix, / qui veut faire ici-bas ton royaume.

4. Fais-moi t'aimer, Seigneur, dans tous mes frères, / et fais-moi te servir en les ser-
vant.

Haya fisherman melody, Tanzania
As sung by Bishop J. Kibira

1. Kam - pon - der' O - mu - ka - ma, Yan - shu - biz' o - bu -
1. Dem Her - ren will ich fol - gen, der mir das Le - ben

ro - ra. E - go, yan - shu - biz' o bu - ro - ra.
ver - sprach. Ja, Le - ben hat er mir ver - spro - chen.

2. Nainywe barumunaba, / Mwij'abah'oburora. / Ego, mwij'abah'oburora.

3. Omushubiro gurungi, / Guma, taho ekika. / Ego, guma, taho ekika.

4. Omwegesa murungi, / Yanyeges'ekigambo. / Ego, yanyeges'ekigambo.

5. Nag'omururu gwensi, / Gutakukuhemura. / Ego, gutakukuhemura.

6. Tutakebuka rundi, / Ebyoturanagire. / Ego, ebyoturanagire.

7. Katwakubikebuka, / Twakunag'oburora. / Ego, twakunag'oburora.

8. Yesu, nzira kamogo, / Nchuro yemirembe. / Ego, nchuro yemirembe.

9. Omugabo gurungi, / Nigwo ndikwitanira. / Ego, nigwo ndikwitanira.

2. Auch euch, ihr meine Lieben, / wird Gottes Leben geschenkt. / Ja, wahres Leben will Gott geben.

3. Ihr alle habt die Hoffnung, / seid stark und haltet sie fest. / Ja, laßt euch von der Hoffnung halten.

4. Der gute Lehrer Jesus / hat Gottes Wort mich gelehrt. / Ja, er war's, der das Wort mich lehrte.

5. Trenn dich von deiner Habgier, / sie bringt in Schande und Schuld. / Ja, Schande wird sie dir sonst bringen.

6. Was gestern uns beschwert hat, / darf nicht nach rückwärts uns ziehn. / Ja, rück - wärts wollen wir nicht gehen.

7. Denn leben wir nach rückwärts, / geht uns das Leben verlorn. / Ja, sonst verlieren wir das Leben.

8. Die Quelle unsres Lebens, / ist Jesus, Mensch ohne Fehl. / Ja, er ist unsres Lebens Quelle.

9. Mein Leben hat zum Endziel / den Preis, den Gott uns verheißt. / Ja, danach will ich immer streben.

1. *Let me follow the Lord; he has promised me life. Yes, he has promised me life.*
2. *And to you also, my relatives, he wants to give life. Yes, he wants to give life.*
3. *For the sake of the good hope be strong, get involved. Yes, be strong, get involved.*
4. *The good teacher taught me the good word. Yes, he has taught me the good word.*
5. *Throw away your worldly greediness; it will lead you to shame. Yes, it will lead you to shame.*
6. *Let us not turn back to the things we have already denounced. Yes, to the things we have already denounced.*
7. *If we turn back to them, we may lose life. Yes, we may lose life.*
8. *Jesus, the spotless one, is the source of life. Yes, he is the source of life.*
9. *I am striving for the good reward in the end. Yes, for that I am striving.*

Brian Wren, UK

Erik Routley, UK **48**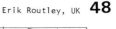

1. Lord God, your love has called us here as we_, by love, for love were made. Your liv - ing_ like - ness still we bear, though marred, dis - ho - noured, dis - o - beyed. We come, with all our heart and mind your call to hear, your_ love _ to find.

2. We come with self-inflicted pains / of broken trust and chosen wrong, / half-free, half-bound by inner chains, / by social forces swept along, / by powers and systems close confined / yet seeking hope for humankind.

3. Lord God, in Christ you call our name / and then receive us as your own / not through some merit, right or claim / but by your gracious love alone. / We strain to glimpse your mercy-seat / and find you kneeling at our feet.

4. Then take the towel, and break the bread, / and humble us, and call us friends. / Suffer and serve till all are fed, / and show how grandly love intends / to work till all creation sings, / to fill all worlds, to crown all things.

5. Lord God, in Christ you set us free / your life to live, your joy to share. / Give us your Spirit's liberty / to turn from guilt and dull despair / and offer all that faith can do / while love is making all things new.

49 Federico J. Pagura, Argentina

Alejandro Núñez Allauca, Perú

1. So - bre es-tas tie - rras que el su - dor re - gó por tan-tos
1. Through-out this earth, sweat-drenched by toil se - vere, through time- less
1. Ü - ber dem Schmerz der un - ter-drück-ten Welt, die Jahr und

si - glos de san-gre y do - lor, ve-mos le - van - tar - se
years of hu - man blood and pain, now we see the sun a -
Tag in Blut und Qual ver - ging, se - hen wir die Son - ne

ya de nue-vo el sol, por - que Dios pro - cla - ma su li - be - ra -
rise with ra-diance clear as our lib - er - a -tion God to us makes
ei - ner neu-en Zeit. Gott schenkt uns die Frei-heit, bricht das Joch ent-

Refrain (faster)

ción. Cris-to es - tá rom - pien-do al fin ca - de - nas de o - pre-
plain. Christ at last as - sun -der breaks op - pres-sion's self-ish
zwei. Chri-stus sprengt die Skla-ven - ket - ten, macht uns end-lich

sión _____; lle-ga a nues - tros pue-blos ple - na re - den - ción.
chain _____, full re-demp - tion for each na - tion now shall reign.
frei _____! Chri-stus sprengt die Skla-ven - ket- ten, macht uns frei!

2. Pueblos cansados de tanto gemir, / bajo su aliento han de revivir. / Nuestros cuerpos y almas viene a restaurar, / trae justicia; El es nuestra paz.

3. Más que otros mundos, quiere El conquistar / la ciudadela de esta humanidad; / quiere a todos darnos nuevo corazón, / donde el odio muera y triunfe el amor.

2. Nations once weary moaned in dull despair; / now through his Spirit they shall soon revive / for he comes our souls and bodies to repair. / He to earth brings peace; his justice makes alive.

3. Not other worlds to conquer he desires, / but the strong fort of this humanity. / Hearts renewed complete within us he inspires / where hate dies and love reigns in pure sanity.

2. Leidendes Volk, erniedrigt und im Zorn, / durch Gottes Atem stehst du wieder auf. / Gott stellt als sein Bild uns Menschen wieder her. / Er verschafft uns Recht, und Frie - den muß entstehn.

3. Gott wünscht uns nicht auf einen fremden Stern, / er braucht uns hier im Hinterhof der Welt. / Liebe zeigt sich da, wo Änderung entsteht. / Er will, daß der Hass zwischen uns Menschen stirbt.

하 늘 나 는 새 를 보 라 농 사 하 지
1. Oh be-hold ___ the fowls of the air, they do not sow,
1. Seht die Vö - gel am Him-mel euch an, seht, sie sä - en

앞 으 며 곡 식 모 아 곡 간 안 에
they do not plough, ga - ther they ___ not, har - vest they not,
und ern-ten nicht, le - gen auch kei-ne Vor - rä - te an,

둘 인 것 이 없 어 도 하 늘 계 신
stock they not the ___ barns ___ and stalls. Heav'n - ly Fa - ther
sam - meln nicht in die Scheu - nen ein. Doch es er - nährt,

아 버 지 가 그 이 먹 여 주 시 니 먹 고
feeds ___ them well, aren't we so much bet - ter than they? Nev - er
speist sie und tränkt eu - er Va - ter in ___ der Höh! Seid ihr

마 실 것 을 위 해 아 무 염 려 말 아 라
wor - ry what you may eat; nev - er wor - ry ___ what you may drink.
selbst denn nicht mehr wert als sie? Dar - um sorgt um das Le - ben nicht.

2. 들 에피는 꽃을보라 / 길쌈수고 안해도 / 솔로몬의 외복보다 / 더욱 아름답도다 /
아궁속에 던질풀도 / 그 이입히 시거든 / 사랑하는 자녀들을 / 입히시지 않으랴 .

3. 너는먼저 주의나라 / 주의 의를 구하라 / 하나님이 모든것을 / 너희에게 주시리 /
내일일을 생각하고 / 미리 염려 말아라 / 오늘일만 생각하고 / 있는힘을 다하라 .

2. O behold the lilies in fields, / they do not toil, they do not spin. / Not the glory
of Solomon / dims the wonder they display. / Heav'nly Father clothes them well, / e'en
those who don't know his love. / Never worry what you may wear; / won't he clothe his
lovèd child?

3. Seek you first the kingdom of God; / seek you first the love of God. / Heav'nly Father through his love / gives you all your daily needs. / For tomorrow, take you no heed /
for the cares and worry it brings. / Take heed for the cares of today; / leave your
heart and mind to him.

2. Seht die Blumen auf blühendem Feld, / seht, sie arbeiten, spinnen nicht. / Salomo
trotz der herrlichen Pracht / trug kein schöneres Kleid als sie. / Wenn Gott das Gras
aufblühen läßt, / das doch dürr wird und verbrennt, / wird er dann sich nicht kümmern
um euch? / Warum ist euer Glaube klein?

3. Stellt euch endlich auf Gottes Reich ein / und auf seine Gerechtigkeit. / Wenn ihr
so tut, wie Gott von euch will, / gibt er alles, was euch noch fehlt. / Sorgt darum
nicht, was morgen wird. / Fragt nicht, was die Zukunft bringt, / denn der morgige Tag
sorgt für sich. / Lasten tragt ihr schon heut' genug!

Federico J. Pagura, Argentina   Homero Perera, Argentina

1. Por-que El en - tró en el mun-do y en la his - to - ria; por-que El que-
1. Be-cause he came in - to our world and sto - ry, be-cause he
1. In un - ser Le - ben, in un-sre Ge -schich- te ist er ge -

bró el si-len-cio y la a-go - ní - a; por-que lle-nó la tie - rra de su
heard our si-lence and our sor - row, be-cause he filled the whole world with his
kom -men, sie mit uns zu tei - len, und hat das Schwei-gen, hat die Angst zer-

glo - ria; por-que fue luz en nues-tra no - che frí - a; por-que El na-
glo - ry, and came to light the dark-ness of our mor - row, be-cause his
bro-chen und un-sre Dun - kel-heit in Licht ver-wan-delt. In ei - nem

ció en un pe - se - bre os - cu - ro; por-que El vi - vió sem-bran-do a-mor y
birth was in a dark - ened cor - ner, be-cause he lived pro-claim-ing life and
un - be-kann- ten Stall ge - bo - ren, um Lie - be aus-zu-säen und neu - es

vi - da; por-que par - tió los co - ra - zo - nes du - ros y le - van-
love__, be-cause he quick-ened hearts that had been dorm-ant, and lift - ed
Le - ben, er-starr- te Her-zen end - lich zu er - wei-chen und die zu

Refrain

tó las al - mas 'a - ba - ti - das. Por e - so es que hoy te - ne - mos es - pe-
those whose lives had been down-trod-den. So we to - day have hope and ex-pec-
stüt - zen, die am Bo-den lie -gen. Und dar-um sind wir heu - te vol-ler

ran - za; por e - so es que hoy lu - cha - mos con por - fí - a; por
ta - tion, so we to - day can strug - gle with con - vic - tion, so
Hoff - nung, und dar - um kämp - fen wir heut' oh - ne Zit - tern, und

e - so es que hoy mi - ra - mos con con - fian - za, el por - ve-
we to - day can trust we have a fu - ture, so we have
dar - um blik - ken wir heut' voll Ver - trau - en, in ei - ne

140

nir, en es - ta tie-rra	mí - a. Por	e - so es que hoy te - ne - mos es - pe-	
hope in this our world of	tears____. So	we to - day have hope and ex - pec-	
neu - e Zu-kunft für uns	al - le. Und	dar - um sind wir heu-te vol - ler	

ran - za; por	e - so es que hoy lu - cha - mos con por - fí - a; por		
ta - tion, so	we to - day can strug - gle with con - vic-tion, so		
Hoff - nung, und	dar - um kämp - fen wir heut' oh - ne Zit-tern, und		

e - so es que hoy mi - ra - mos con con - fian - za,	el por - ve - nir		
we to - day can trust we have a fu - ture,	so we have hope		
dar - um blik - ken wir heut' voll Ver - trau - en	auf das, was kommt		

1-2 Dm 7   Stz. 3 from %   **3** Dm 7

2. Por-que a - ta - - nir_____.
2. Be-cause he
2. Ge-gen den

2. Porque atacó a ambiciosos mercaderes / y denunció maldad e hipocresía; / porque exaltó a los niños, las mujeres, / y rechazó a los que de orgullo ardían. / Porque El cargó la cruz de nuestras penas / y saboreó la hiel de nuestros males; / porque aceptó sufrir nuestra condena / y así morir por todos los mortales.

3. Porque una aurora vió su gran victoria / sobre la muerte, el miedo, las mentiras; / ya nada puede detener su historia, / ni de su Reino eterno la venida.

2. Because he drove the merchants from the temple, / denouncing evil and hypocrisy, / because he raised up little ones and women, / and put down all the mighty from their seats, / because he bore the cross for our wrongdoings, / and understood our failings and our weakness, / because he suffered from our condemnation / and then he died for every mortal creature.

3. Because of victory one morning early, / when he defeated death and fear and sorrow, / so nothing can hold back his mighty story / nor his eternal kingdom tomorrow.

2. Gegen den Ehrgeiz der Geschäftemacher / hat er gekämpft, und gegen jede Lüge, / den Frauen, Kindern eignen Wert gegeben, / aber die stolz und hart sind abgewiesen. / Er trug mit uns das Kreuz all unsrer Schmerzen / und litt wie wir die Qual all unsrer Übel, / war selbst bereit, der Menschen Schuld zu teilen, / um so den Tod für immer zu besiegen.

3. Weil unsre Welt die Zeichen seiner Macht sah / über den Tod, die Angst und alle Lügen, / ist heute schon sein Wirken unaufhaltsam / und wird auf Dauer niemals unterliegen.

1. Who are we__ who stand and sing____? We are his Peo- ple.
What this bread and wine we bring __? Food for his Peo- ple.
1. Wer sind wir__, die fei - ern, sin - gen? Volk Got-tes sind wir.
Was sind Brot und Wein, die wir brin-gen? Mahl sei-nes Vol- kes.

As once with twelve he spake, poured wine and bread did break; he now with
Wie er die zwölf an-sprach, Wein ein - goß und Brot brach,wählt er jetzt

us will make a faith-ful__ Peo - ple. be his__ Peo - ple.
uns da -nach zum Volk sei-ner Treu- e. uns zum Volk Got - tes.

2. What command does he impart / to us his People? / Soul and strength and mind and heart; / serve me, my People. / As God in Christ came low, / our world and work to know; / to life he bids us go / to be his People.

3. Who are we who say one Creed? We are his People. / What the word we hear and read ? / Word of his People. / Through time, in every race, / from earth to farthest space, / we with our God's good grace / will be his People.

2. Was hat er uns aufgetragen, / uns, dem Volk Gottes? / "Freut euch, seid an allen Tagen / Volk, das mir gern dient." / Gott ward in Christus klein, / um allen nah zu sein, / lädt uns ins Leben ein, / sein Volk dort zu werden.

3. Wer sind wir, wenn wir bekennen? / Volk Gottes sind wir./Vom Wort Gottes nicht zu tren-nen. / Wort seines Volkes. / Geschlechter jeder Zeit, / ob erdnah, sternenweit / werden durch sein Geleit / mit uns zum Volk Gottes.

Fred Kaan, UK

Jamaican folk song **53**
Adapt. Doreen Potter, Jamaica

1. Let us tal - ents and tongues em - ploy, reach- ing out with a
1. Auf, bringt Ga - ben und Lob her- bei, daß die Freu- de weit

shout of joy: bread is bro - ken, the wine is poured,
hör - bar sei: Brot und Wein wer - den aus - ge - teilt,

Christ is spo - ken and seen and heard. Je - sus lives a - gain,
Chri - stus gibt, was uns hilft und heilt. Tod hält Je - sus nicht,

earth can breathe a - gain, pass the Word a - round: loaves a - bound!
Er - de lebt im Licht, schickt den Ruf hin- aus: Kommt, teilt aus!

2. Christ is able to make us one, / at his table he sets the tone, / teaching people to live to bless, / love in word and in deed express. / Jesus lives again...

3. Jesus calls us in, sends us out / bearing fruit in a world of doubt, / gives us love to tell, bread to share: / God-immanuel everywhere! / Jesus lives again...

2. Christus hilft uns zur Einigkeit, / spricht am Tisch das Gebot der Zeit, / lehrt das Leben als Segen sehn, / Liebe muß in der Tat bestehn./Tod hält Jesus nicht...

3. Jesus ruft uns und sendet aus, / Frucht zu tragen in jedes Haus, / Brot der Liebe für jeden Fall: / Gott ist mit uns und überall. / Tod hält Jesus nicht...

54 Anders Frostenson, Sweden   Olle Widestrand, Sweden

1. Lå - gor - na är mång - a ___ ljus - et är ett ___ lju - set
1. Man - y are the light-beams ___ from the one light. Our one
1. Strah - len bre - chen vie - le ___ aus ei - nem Licht. Un - ser
1. Mu - chos res-plan - do - res ___, só -lo u - na luz: es la

Je - sus Kris - tus ___ lå - gor - na är mång - a ___
light is Je - sus ___. Man - y are the light-beams ___
Licht heißt Chri - stus ___. Strah - len bre - chen vie - le ___
luz de Cris - to ___. Mu - chos res-plan - do - res ___,

lju - set är ett vi är ett i ho - nom ___.
from the one light; we are one in Christ ___.
aus ei - nem Licht-und wir sind eins durch ihn ___.
só -lo u - na luz que nos ha - ce u - no ___.

2. Grenarna är många stammen är en / stammen - Jesus Kristus / grenarna är många stammen är en / vi är ett i honom.

3. Gåvorna är många kärleken en / finns i Jesus Kristus / gåvorna är många kärleken en / vi är ett i honom.

4. Tjänsterna är många Anden är en / Jesu Kristi Ande / tjänsterna är många Anden är en / vi är ett i honom.

5. Lemmarna är många kroppen är en / Jesu Kristi kyrka / lemmarna är många kroppen är en / vi är ett i honom.

2. Many are the branches of the one tree. / Our one tree is Jesus. / Many are the branches of the one tree; / we are one in Christ.

3. Many are the gifts giv'n, love is all one. / Love's the gift of Jesus. / Many are the gifts giv'n, love is all one; / we are one in Christ.

4. Many ways to serve God, the Spirit is one; / servant spirit of Jesus. / Many ways to serve God, the Spirit is one; / we are one in Christ.

5. Many are the members, the body is one; / members all of Jesus. / Many are the members, the body is one; / we are one in Christ.

2. Zweige wachsen viele aus einem Stamm. / Unser Stamm heißt Christus. / Zweige wachsen viele aus einem Stamm - / und wir sind eins durch ihn.

3. Gaben gibt es viele, Liebe nur eine. / Liebe schenkt uns Christus. / Gaben gibt es viele, Liebe nur eine - / und wir sind eins durch ihn.

4. Dienste leben viele aus einem Geist, / Geist von Jesus Christus. / Dienste leben viele aus einem Geist - / und wir sind eins durch ihn.

5. Glieder sind es viele, doch nur ein Leib. / Wir sind Glieder Christi. / Glieder sind es viele, doch nur ein Leib - / und wir sind eins durch ihn.

2. Muchas son las ramas, un árbol hay: / y su tronco es Cristo. / Muchas son las ramas, un tronco hay / y en él somos uno.

3. Muchos son los dones, uno el amor: / el amor de Cristo. / Muchos son los dones, uno el amor / que nos hace uno.

4. Muchas las tareas, uno el sentir: / el sentir de Cristo. / Muchas las tareas, uno el sentir / que nos hace uno.

5. Muchos son los miembros, un cuerpo hay: / ese cuerpo es Cristo. / Muchos son los miembros, un cuerpo hay, / y en él somos uno.

Refrain

E - дин-ство Це - рквъ, чтоб е - дин был мир_____,
E - din-stvo Tse - rkvi, shtob e - din byl mir_____,
U - ni-ty of the Church_____, u - ni-ty of the world_____,
Ein-heit für dei - ne Kir - che, Ein-heit für dei - ne Welt_____,

Fine

Спра - вед - ли - вый по - иск, Бо-же, дай нам Ду - хом Сил.
spra - ved - li - vyi po - isk, Bo-je, dai nam Du - khom Sil.
full - ness of life in jus - tice_____, give us, God, the Lord.
Le - ben er-füllt durch Recht und Lie - be_____, gib, Herr, un - ser Gott!

1. Пре-свя-та-я Тро - и-ца есть_____ жиз-ни всей ви - на_____;
1. Pre-svia-ta-ia Tro - i-tsa est'_____ jiz-ni vsei vi - na_____;
1. U - ni-ty in Je - sus Christ is the source of life and peace_____,
1. Ein - heit in Chri-stus ist Quell des Le - bens und des Frie -dens.

D.C.

Дай_____ сил, чтоб жизнь в ми - ре_____ бы - ла спа - се - на.
dai_____ sil, shtob jizn' v mi - re_____ by - la spa - se - na.
give_____ us, O_____ Lord, your_____ mer - cy and your grace.
Herr_____, sei uns_____ gnä - dig, er - barm dich ü - ber uns.

2. Через Христа Логоса, нашего Творца, / мир веди, о Боже, к счастию венца.

2. Tcherez Christa Logosa, naschego Tvortsa, / mir vedi, o Boje, k sĉastiiu ventsa.

2. Let Christ's salvation transform a world in strife. / And to all creation bring his joy and life.

2. Mit Gottes Schöpfung und allem Leben dieser Welt: / macht Christi Rettertat bei jung und alt bekannt!

56 T. Herbert O'Driscoll, Canada — Henry Hugh Bancroft, Canada

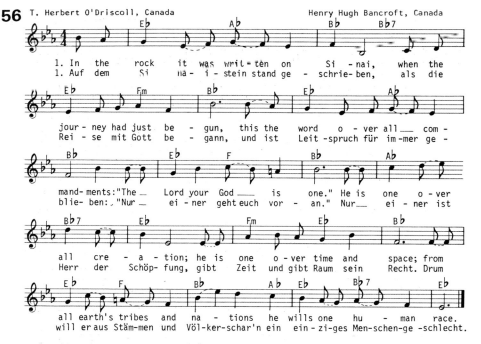

1. In the rock it was writ-ten on Si - nai, when the jour-ney had just be - gun, this the word o - ver all___ com - mand-ments: "The ___ Lord your God ___ is one." He is one o - ver all cre - a - tion; he is one o - ver time and space; from all earth's tribes and na - tions he wills one hu - man race.

1. Auf dem Si na - i - stein stand ge - schrie-ben, als die Rei - se mit Gott be - gann, und ist Leit -spruch für im-mer ge - blie- ben: "Nur ___ ei - ner geht euch vor - an." Nur ___ ei - ner ist Herr der Schöp- fung, gibt Zeit und gibt Raum sein Recht. Drum will er aus Stäm-men und Völ-ker-schar'n ein ein - zi-ges Men-schen-ge -schlecht.

2. In the room where wine was offered / and the hands of a King broke bread, / he spoke of a cross to be suffered / and a rising from the dead. / That wine and bread are a token / till aeons of time are done; / to a people divided and broken / he wills that his Church be one.

3. What was heard in the thunder of Sinai, / what was seen in the Saviour's face, / is alive and among us as Spirit / and touches us by grace. / For a thousand tongues are speaking, / and the wind and the fire begun / proclaim to humanity seeking / that God and his people are one.

4. When the pain of a planet appalls us / and the hope of a kingdom dies, / from the mount of the law God calls us, / from the mount of the cross he cries. / Though his wounds are the warring nations, / the starving child his own, / he reigns in expectation; / he wills that his world be one.

2. In dem Saal, wo der Wein sich bereit fand, / und wo Jesus selbst brach das Brot, / sprach er klar von dem Kreuz, das bevorstand, / vom Leben auch aus dem Tod. / Das Mahl ist sein Lebenszeichen, / bis Welten vergangen sind. / Vom Volk, das zertrennt und zerbrochen ist, / will er, daß es Einigkeit findt'.

3. Was im Donnersturm Sinais aufklang, / was in Jesu Gesicht erschien, / wirkt als Geist unter uns neuen Anfang, / in Freiheit läßt er uns ziehn. / Denn tausende Sprachen sprechen, / was Wind und was Feuer meint, / verkünden dem Volk, das sich sehnt und sucht: / Es sind Gott und Mensch neu vereint.

4. Wenn die Leiden der Welt uns entsetzen, / Gottes Herrschaft scheint arm und weit, / ruft der Herr uns vom Berg in Gesetzen, / vom Berg des Kreuzes er schreit. / Sein Schmerz sind die Kriege der Völker, / das hungernde Kind ist seins, / doch herrscht er, indem er noch immer hofft, / und will, seine Welt werde eins.

Antonio Morales

1. Va - lles-nin - ta lo -mas-nin - ta ta-quis-pa ri - saj,
1. Por los va - lles y los ce - rros yo can-tan-do voy,
1. Through the by - ways and the high-ways, joy-ful - ly I sing,
1. Par les che -mins, plaines et monts ___ , joy- eux, je ___ chante.
1. In den Tä - lern, auf den Hö - hen sin - ge ich mein Lied,

Se - ñor Je - sus-niy wa - kay - cha - ha - wan, Se- ñor Je - sus - niy
mi Se - ñor Je -sús pues con- mi-go es-tá, mi Con- so - la - dor,
moun-tains e -cho -ing, prais-es to the King. He my Shep-herd is;
Jé - sus le Sei-gneur mar -che de-vant moi. Que crain-drais-je en-core
Je - sus, mei-nem Herrn, der mich nie ver-läßt. Er be - hü - tet mich

ño - ka - wan cas - han. Mu - na - cu - wan per - do - na - wan,
él me cui - da - rá. El me a - ma y me cui - da,
he will walk with me. Je -sus loves me, guides and feeds me.
il est a - vec moi! Il me con - duit, me tient la main,
so, daß mir nichts fehlt. Je -sus liebt mich, lei - tet, speist mich,

sal - va - cu - wan call - pa - cha - wan, rej - si - ni mu -
me a - lien - ta y me guar - da, re - co - noz - co
He pro - tects and he will lead me. God's love speaks to
si je chan - celle, il me re - tient. Je chan -terai son
er be - schützt und führt mich täg - lich. Lie - be holt mich

na - cuy - nin - ta may - lla - pi - pis ño - ka - wan.
su a - mor ___ don - de - quie - ra que an-de yo.
me each day ___ as I walk a - long my way.
grand a - mour ___ , tel au - jour-d'hui et tou - jours.
stän - dig ein ___ , will stets mein Be - glei- ter sein.

2. Tutas llaquiska cashajtiy, / Pay cusichiwan. / Pay yanapawan, / sumaj Salvador. / Pay yanapawan, / sumaj Salvador.

2. En mis noches de tristeza / me consolará, / me ayudará / mi fiel Salvador. / Me ayudará / mi fiel Salvador.

2. In the nights of pain and sadness, / on him I depend, / love and care he'll send, / he's my faithful friend. / He my comfort is; / I can trust in him.

2. Au temps sombre du désespoir, / Jésus est présent. / Il sera toujours / mon Consola - teur. / En lui, je puis tout, / il me fortifie.

2. In den Nächten meiner Trauer / wird er mir zum Trost, / kümmert sich um mich. / Treu steht er mir bei, / als der beste Freund / spricht er mir gut zu.

58

Traditional Hindi melody, India

* "Praise be to you"

148

149

59 Psalm 145:1-3   Casiodoro Cárdenas, Ecuador

1. Te e - xal - ta - ré, mi Dios, mi Rey, y ben - de - ci -
1. I will ex - tol my God, my King, and for - ev - er
1. Je t'e - xal - te - rai, mon Dieu, mon roi, et je bé - ni -
1. Ich will dich lo - ben, Herr, mein Gott. Dei - nem Na - men

ré tu nom - bre e - ter - na - men-te y pa - ra
bless his ho - ly name. Now and for - ev - er I will
rai ton beau nom. Tou - jours et à per - pé - tui -
sin - gen im - mer - dar. Ich will dich rüh - men, du mein

siem - pre. Ca - da dí - a te ben - de - ci - ré, y a - la - ba -
bless him, I will sing the prais - es of the Lord. I will bless his
té____, cha - que jour____ je te bé - ni - rai, et je cé - lé -
Kö - nig, heu - te und in al - le E - wig - keit. Ich will prei - sen

ré tu nom - bre e - ter - na - men-te y pa - ra
name, 0 God my King, now and for - ev - er I will
bre - rai ton nom tou - jours et à per - pé - tui -
dei - nen Na - men. Jauch-zen will ich ganz ohn' Auf -

siem - pre. Gran - de es Je - ho - vá, y dig - no de su -
bless him. Oh how great is the Lord, and wor - thy of all
té____. Très grand est le Sei - gneur et très dig - ne de
hö - ren. O wie groß bist du, Herr, mein Lo - ben ist zu

pre - ma a - la - ban - za; y su gran - de - za es i -
praise and ad - o - ra - tion. Oh how mag - nif - i - cent
su - prê - me lou - an - ge. Que sa gran - deur est____
kläg - lich, dich zu fas - sen. Herr, ich will sin - gen von

nes - cru - ta - ble; ca - da dí - a te ben - de - ci - ré____.
is God's great - ness; I will sing the prais - es of the Lord____.
in - son - da - ble, cha - que jour____ je te bé - ni - rai____.
dei - ner Grö - ße, die in Wahr - heit un - er - meß - lich ist____.

150

1. The God of us all is our Father, he
guides us when we are in danger, he
calls us to honour the stranger.
Great is the Lord, ever adored.

1. Der Gott aller Menschen ist Vater, er
führt und schützt, wenn Gefahr uns bedroht, beruft uns, die Fremden zu ehren.
Groß ist der Herr, hochgelobt.

2. The God of us all is our Mother,/ she teaches us her truth and beauty,/ she shows us a love beyond duty./ Great is the Lord, ever adored.

3. Our God is a Father and Mother,/ surrounding us all with protection,/ to give to the world new direction./ Great is the Lord, ever adored.

2. Der Gott aller Menschen ist Mutter, / sie lehrt uns, Wahrheit und Schönheit zu sehn, / zeigt Liebe, die nicht sich in Pflicht erschöpft. / Groß ist der Herr, hochgelobt!

3. Der Gott, der uns Vater und Mutter ist, / gewährt uns allen ein gutes Geleit, / damit unsre Welt weiss, wohin sie zielt. / Groß ist der Herr, hochgelobt!

Dieter Trautwein, Germany

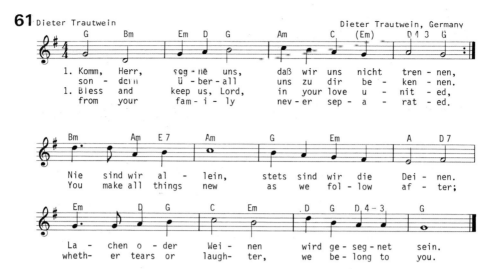

1. Komm, Herr, seg - ne uns, daß wir uns nicht tren - nen,
   son - dern ü - ber - all uns zu dir be - ken - nen.
1. Bless and keep us, Lord, in your love u - nit - ed,
   from your fam - i - ly nev - er sep - a - rat - ed.

Nie sind wir al - lein, stets sind wir die Dei - nen.
You make all things new as we fol - low af - ter;

La - chen o - der Wei - nen wird ge - seg - net sein.
wheth- er tears or laugh- ter, we be - long to you.

2. Keiner kann allein Segen sich bewahren. / Weil du reichlich gibst, müssen wir nicht sparen. / Segen kann gedeihn, wo wir alles teilen, / schlimmen Schaden heilen, lieben und verzeihn.

3. Frieden gabst du schon, Frieden muß noch werden / wie du ihn versprichst uns zum Wohl auf Erden. / Hilf, daß wir ihn tun, wo wir ihn erspähen - / die mit Tränen säen, werden in ihm ruhn.

4. = 1.

2. Blessing shrivels up when your children hoard it; / help us, Lord, to share, for we can afford it: / blessing only grows in the act of sharing, / in a life of caring, love that heals and glows.

3. Fill your world with peace, such as you intended. / Help us prize the earth, love, re-plenish, tend it. / Lord, uplift, fulfil all who sow in sadness: / let them reap with glad-ness, by your kingdom thrilled.

4. = 1.

Jane Parker Huber, USA

USA **62**

1. Je-sus Christ, whose pas-sion claims us, call-ing us from age to age,
by your grace, your own name names us mak-ing rich our___ her-it-age.
Sum-mon now your peo-ple, wan-der-ing, east and west, and___ south and north.
Shape our ac-tion and our pon-der-ing. Meet us___ here, then send us forth.

2. Life of life and spur of action, / Christ, the heartbeat and the breath, / keep us from each feud or faction / leading us to certain death.

We confess our wrong intentions. / Now replace them with your will. / Wash us clean of all pretensions. / May your grace our actions fill.

3. Light to brighten this world's sorrows / breaking through the dark of night, / Oh, illu-mine our tomorrows. / Show us futures clear and bright.

God Incarnate, still redeeming / all relationships on earth, / match our deeds to our best dreaming. / Give our visions truth and worth.

4. So we sing of life confronting, / even overcoming, death. / All our searching, all our hunting, / yields us not a single breath.

Only Christ has won the glory: / songs and praises are unfurled / like a banner with the story - / Jesus Christ, Life of the World!

153

Sources of prayers
Sources des prières
Quellenangaben für die Gebete
Procedencia de las oraciones

We wish to thank all those who have granted permission for the use of prayers in this book. We have made every effort to trace and identify them correctly and to secure the necessary permissions for reprinting. If we have erred in any way in the acknowledgments, or have unwittingly infringed any copyright, we apologize sincerely. We would be glad to make the necessary corrections in subsequent editions of this book.

3. Isa. 55:1-3, 6; Ps. 42:2: Sixth Assembly Worship Committee.

4. Worship Committee.

5. Taizé community, France.

6. Based on *New Orders of the Mass in India,* as in Asia Sunday prayer leaflet, 1982, CCA, Singapore.

7. Episcopal Church, USA (slightly adapted).

8. Prayer from West Africa by Fritz Pawelzik, *I Sing Your Praise All the Day Long,* Friendship Press, New York, 1967.

11. Rom. 8:18-23 and Rev. 21:1: Worship Committee.

12. Worship Committee.

13. Mark 6:34-36, John 8:9-11, Luke 10:31, John 19:1-2, 9-10, Luke 4:18: Worship Committee. Based on the meditation in *Worship Handbook,* Seventh Assembly of the Christian Conference of Asia, Singapore, 1981.

14. Edmund Jones, *Worship and Wonder,* Galliard, Great Yarmouth, UK, 1971.

15. WCC-Commission on the Churches' Participation in Development, Newsletter, January 1982 (adapted).

16. Intercession from the Pacific Conference of Churches (adapted).

19. Gen. 1:1-3, 31, John 1:14, 16, 2 Cor. 5:17-18, Gal. 5:1, 25: Worship Committee.

20. Joan Puls, School Sisters of St Francis.

21. Worship Committee.

22. "A Form of Prayer", WCC (adapted).

23. Prayer from the Sheffield conference, 1981, Community of Women and Men in the Church study, WCC.

24. Worship Committee.

25. *Byzantine Book of Prayer,* Byzantine Seminary Press, Pittsburg, and Alleluia Press, Allendale, NJ, 1976, p. 26.

28. 1 John 4:7, Col. 3:15, Eph. 2:14-22, 4:3-6: Worship Committee.

29. *Morning, Noon and Night: Prayer and Meditations from the Third World,* ed. John Carden, CMS, London, 1976.

30. Elsa Tamez, in *International Review of Mission,* October 1982 (adapted).

31. Art Solomon, Ojibway Native Canadian prayer from the message of the Mauritius Assembly preparatory meeting, January 1983.

32. *For All God's People: Ecumenical Prayer Cycle,* WCC, Geneva, 1978 (adapted).

33. Based on the prayer "The Ministry of Reconciliation", in *Worship Now,* compiled by David Cairns et al., St Andrews Press, Edinburgh, 1972.

34. *Contemporary Prayers for Public Worship,* ed. Caryl Micklem, SCM Press, London, 1967.

35. *Risk,* WCC, Geneva, Vol. 11, Nos. 2-3, 1975, p. 69.

38. Source unknown.

39. Statement by the United Church of Canada.

42-43. Source unknown.

44. Based on a prayer by Robert H. Adams Jr, *A Traveller's Prayer Book,* The Upper Room, Nashville.

45. *Contemporary Prayers for Public Worship, op. cit.*

46. From an ecumenical committee for the participation of Christians of other churches in the 41st Eucharistic Congress, Philadelphia, 1976.

47-48. Source unknown.

49. *Risk,* WCC, Geneva, Vol. 11, Nos. 2-3, 1975, p. 25.

50. "Prayer for Peace", 1982.

Sources of music
Sources des cantiques et répons
Quellenangaben für die Musik
Procedencia de la música

We wish to thank all those who have granted permission for the use of music in this book. We have made every effort to trace and identify the items correctly and to secure the necessary permissions for reprinting. If we have erred in any way in the acknowledgments, or have unwittingly infringed any copyright, we apologize sincerely. We would be glad to make the necessary corrections in subsequent editions of this book.

Abbreviations/Abréviations/Abkürzungen/Abreviaturas

Adapt. = Adapted by
Arr.   = Arranged by
Tr.   = Translated

M: Melody/Mélodie/Melodie/Melodia
O: Original
T: Text/Texte/Text/Texto
d: German/allemand/deutsch/alemán
e: English/anglais/englisch/inglés
f: French/français/französisch/francés
s: Spanish/espagnol/spanisch/español

Italics indicate paraphrases which are not singable.

Les passages en italique ont été traduits sans être adaptés à la musique.

Die kursiv gedruckten Texte sind Übersetzungen, bei denen die Melodie nicht berücksichtigt wurde.

Los pasajes en letra bastardilla se han traducido pero no se han adaptado a la música.

No.	Writer, translator, composer, arranger	Copyright holder or controller	Source
p. 4	T: (O:e) from Psalm 41(42). M: I-to Loh	M+T(e) I-to Loh	Worship Book
p. 36	T: (O:f) from Psalm 129(130) (e) The Grail. M: Joseph Gelineau	M: Secrétariat des Editeurs de Fiches Musicales, Paris, Used by permission.	Vingt-quatre Psaumes et un cantique
p. 45	T: (O:e) from John 1. M: Dawn Ross	M+T(e) WCC	Worship Book
p. 64	T: (O:e) Fritz Baltruweit (f) Max Thurian (d) Dieter Trautwein (s) Pablo Sosa. M: Fritz Baltruweit	M+T(e) F. Baltruweit (f) WCC (d) D. Trautwein (s) P. Sosa	Worship Book
1	T: (O:e) Doreen Potter (f) Etienne de Peyer (d) Reinhild Traitler. M: Doreen Potter	M+T(e) D. Potter (f) E. de Peyer (d) R. Traitler	M+T(e) Now, Methodist Church, London (f,d) Worship Book
2	T: (O:bassa, +e, f) Bayiga Bayiga (d) D. Trautwein (s) P. Sosa. M: Bayiga Bayiga	M+T(O,e,f) Bayiga Bayiga (d) D. Trautwein (s) P. Sosa	Worship Book
3	T: (O:d) Josef Metternich team (e) Evelyn Talbot-Ponsonby (f) E. de Peyer. M: Peter Janssens	M+T(d,e) Peter Janssens Musik Verlag, Telgte, FRG. Used by permission. (f) E. de Peyer	M+T(d) Wir haben einen Traum (e) Break Down the Walls (f) Worship Book
4	T: (O:s, +e) Psalm 133(134) arr. P. Sosa (d) D. Trautwein, M: P. Sosa	M+T(s,e) P. Sosa (d) D. Trautwein	M+T(s) Cancionero Abierto I, ISE-DET, Buenos Aires (e) International Songbook (d) Worship Book
5	M+T(O:shona) Patrick Matsike-nyiri	M+T(O) United Methodist Church Music Service, Mutambara CPS Box 61, Cashel, Zimbabwe	Ndwiyo Dzechechi Dzevhu I
6	T (O:latin). M: Jacques Berthier	M: Les Presses de Taizé, 71250 Taizé, France, also G.I.A., Chicago, Collins,	Chants de Taizé III: Chanter l'Esprit

No.	Writer, translator, composer, arranger	Copyright holder or controller	Source
		London, and Christophorus-Verlag Herder, Freiburg. Used by permission.	
7	T: tr.(f) anonymous. M: Greek Orthodox liturgy		
8	T: (O:coptic) (e) Martha A. Roy. M: Coptic Orthodox liturgy		
9	T: tr.(e) adapted from traditional Hindi text by I-to Loh. M: Bhajan melody, arr. I-to Loh	M+T(e) I-to Loh	*Hymns from the Four Winds*
10	T: (O:s) Ulises Torres (e) Alvin Schutmaat (d) Carlos Corvalan, D. Trautwein. M: Chilean folk melody	T: (s) U. Torres (e) A. Schutmaat (d) C. Corvalan, D. Trautwein	M+T(s) *Cancionero Abierto I* (e,d) Worship Book
11	T (O:greek). M: Jacques Berthier	M: Les Presses de Taizé, 71250 Taizé, France, also G.I.A., Chicago, Collins, London, and Christophorus-Verlag Herder, Freiburg. Used by permission.	*Chants de Taizé III: Chanter l'Esprit*
12	T: (O:chinese). M: I-to Loh	M+T(O) I-to Loh	*Le-pai Gak-chiong*
13	T:(O:indonesian, +e) Sutarno (f) E. de Peyer (d) D. Trautwein (s) P. Sosa. M: Javanese melody, arr. Sutarno	M+T (O,e) Sutarno (f) E. de Peyer (d) D. Trautwein (s) P. Sosa	Worship Book
14	T: (O:greek). M: Russian Orthodox liturgy		

No.	Writer, translator, composer, arranger	Copyright holder or controller	Source
15	T: (O:greek). M: Russian Orthodox liturgy		
16	T: (O:roumanian). M: Ghelasie Basarabeanul		
17	T: (O:greek). M: Greek Orthodox liturgy		
18	T: (O:s, +e) from Matthew 6, arr. P. Sosa (f) Dawn Ross (d) D. Trautwein. M: P. Sosa	M+T(s,e) P. Sosa (f) WCC (d) D. Trautwein	M+T(s) *Cancionero Abierto III* (e) *Your Kingdom Come*, WCC (f,d) Worship Book
19	T: (O:e) from Psalm 26 (27). M: Jacques Berthier	M: Les Presses de Taizé, 71250 Taizé, France. Used by permission.	*Chants de Taizé V: Chants nouveaux en diverses langues*
20	T: (O:d) from Isaiah 40, arr. Volker Ochs. M: Volker Ochs	M+T(d) Volker Ochs	Worship Book
21	T: (O:indonesian, +e) Sutarno (f) E. de Peyer (d) D. Trautwein. M: Javanese melody, arr. Sutarno	M+T(O,e) Sutarno (f) E. de Peyer (d) D. Trautwein	Worship Book
22	T: (O:shona). M: Abraham Maraire	M+T(O) United Methodist Church Music Service, Mutambara CPS Box 61, Cashel, Zimbabwe	*Ndwiyo Dzechechi Dzevhu I*
23	T: (O:s, +e) P. Sosa (d) D. Trautwein	M+T(s,e) P. Sosa (d) D. Trautwein	M+T(s) *Cancionero Abierto I* (e,d) Worship Book
24	T: (O:mungaka) (f) Bayiga Bayiga (d) Irmhild Lyonga, D. Trautwein (s) P. Sosa		M+T(O) *Children's Songs from Around the World*, LWF (e,f,d,s) Worship Book
25	T: (O:e) from Luke 4, arr. Jim Strathdee (s) Katherine E. Strathdee. M: Jim Strathdee	M+T(e,s) Desert Flower Music, Ridgecrest, California. Used by permission.	*Light of the World*

No.	Writer, translator, composer, arranger	Copyright holder or controller	Source
26	T: (O:ga) from Deuteronomy 6. M: Ghanaian melody, arr. I-to Loh		Worship Book
27	T: (O:d) from Philippians 2, arr. D. Trautwein (e) Len Lythgoe (f) E. de Peyer	M+T(d) D. Trautwein (e) L. Lythgoe (f) E. de Peyer	Worship Book
28	T: (O:ga) (e, d) D. Trautwein, Joseph Quartey. M: Ghanaian melody	T(e+d) D. Trautwein, J. Quartey. M: Asempa Publishers, Box 919, Accra	T(e,d) Worship Book. M: *Ghana Praise*
29	T: (O:roumanian) (e) anonymous. M: Roumanian Orthodox liturgy		Worship Book
30	T: (O:shona). M: Patrick Matsikenyiri	M+T(O) United Methodist Church Music Service, Mutambara CPS Box 61, Cashel, Zimbabwe	
31	T: tr.(e) anonymous. M: Betty Pulkingham	M: Celebration Services (International) Ltd., Cathedral of the Isles, Millport, Isle of Cumbrae KA28 OHE, Scotland. All rights reserved. Used by permission.	*The King of Glory*
32	T: (O:latin) from Psalm 117(118). M: Jacques Berthier	M: Les Presses de Taizé, 71250 Taizé, France, also G.I.A., Chicago, Collins, London, and Christophorus-Verlag Herder, Freiburg. Used by permission.	*Chants de Taizé IV: Laudate Dominum*
33	T: (O:latin). M: Jacques Berthier	M: Les Presses de Taizé, 71250 Taizé, France, also G.I.A., Chicago, Collins, London, and Christophorus-Verlag Herder, Freiburg. Used by permission.	*Chants de Taizé II: Chanter le Christ*

No.	Writer, translator, composer, arranger	Copyright holder or controller	Source
34	T: (O:hebrew) from Micah 4 (e) D. Trautwein (d) Friedrich Karl Barth, D. Trautwein (s) P. Sosa	T: (e) D. Trautwein (d) Burkhardt-haus-Laetare Verlag, Gelnhausen. Used by permission. (s) P. Sosa	M+T(d) *Frankfurter Lieder* (e,s) Worship Book
35	T: (O:greek) from Psalm 33(34). M: Greek Orthodox liturgy		
36	M+T (fijian, e) As sung in Fiji		T(fijian) Worship Book
37	M: Jacques Berthier	M: Les Presses de Taizé, 71250 Taizé, France, also G.I.A., Chicago, and Collins, London. Used by permission.	*Chants de Taizé IV: Laudate Dominum*
38	M: Hansruedi Willisegger	M: Theologischer Verlag, Zürich. Used by permission.	*Kumbaya – Oekumenisches Jugendgesangbuch*
39	T: (O:e) Jane Parker Huber. M: *Trente-quatre psaumes de David,* Geneva, 1551	T: (e) Jane Parker Huber	T: (e) Worship Book. M: *Lutheran Book of Worship*
40	T: (O:d) D. Trautwein (e) L. Lythgoe (f) E. de Peyer (s) P. Sosa. M: Herbert Beuerle (revised 1983)	T: (d) D. Trautwein (e) L. Lythgoe (f) E. de Peyer (s) P. Sosa. M: Verlag Singende Gemeinde, Wuppertal. Used by permission.	T: (d, e, f, s) Worship Book. M: *Frankfurter Lieder*
41	M+T(e,f) R. Burn Purdon	M+T(e,f) R. Burn Purdon	Worship Book
42	T: (O:portuguese) Jaci C. Maraschin (e) L. Lythgoe. M: Jaci C. Maraschin	M+T(O) Jaci C. Maraschin (e) L. Lythgoe	Worship Book
43	T (O:e) Sister Lauretta Mather (d) D. Trautwein. M: Sister Lauretta Mather	M+T(e) Sister Lauretta Mather (d) D. Trautwein	Worship Book

No.	Writer, translator, composer, arranger	Copyright holder or controller	Source
44	M+T(O:f) Youth group of Eglise Evangélique en Nouvelle Calédonie et aux Iles Loyauté, Noumea		Worship Book
45	T: (O:s) Mortimer Arias (e) L. Lythgoe (f) E. de Peyer (d) Friedrich Karl Barth. M: Antonio Auza	T: (s) M. Arias (e) L. Lythgoe (f) E. de Peyer (d) F.K. Barth. M: Antonio Auza	M+T(s) Cancionero Abierto IV (e,f,d) Worship Book
46	T: (O:e) Walter Farquharson (f) E. de Peyer. M: Ron Klusmeier	M+T(e) Frederick Harris Music Co. Ltd, Oakville, Ont. Used by permission. (f) E. de Peyer	M+T(e) Worship the Lord (f) Worship Book
47	T: (O:kihaya) Ernest Kalembo (d) D. Trautwein. M: Haya fishermen melody, arr. D. Trautwein	M+T(O) Evangelical Lutheran Church in Tanzania, Northwestern Diocese, Bukoba (d) D. Trautwein	M+T(O) Empoya—Hymns, Liturgy and Catechism in the Haya Language (d) Worship Book
48	T: (O:e) Brian Wren. M: Erik Routley	T: (e) Oxford University Press, London, and Hope Publishing Company, Carol Stream, Illinois. M: Hope Publishing Company. Used by permission	New Church Praise
49	T: (O:s) Federico J. Pagura (e) Delbert Asay (d) Arturo Blatezky, Gerlinde Fischer, Fritz Rohrer. M: Alejandro Núñez Allauca	T: (s) F. J. Pagura (e) D. Asay (d) A. Blatezky, G. Fischer, F. Rohrer. M: A. Núñez Allauca	M+T(s) Cancionero Abierto I (e) Worship Book (d) Lieder der Einheit
50	T: tr.(korean) anonymous (e) Chang Pil-Wha (d) D. Trautwein. M: Nah Young-Soo	T: (e) Chang Pil-Wha (d) D. Trautwein. M: Nah Young-Soo	M+T(O) Songs for Tomorrow, Korea Christian Academy, Seoul (e,d) Worship Book
51	T: (O:s) Federico J. Pagura (e) L. Lythgoe (d) Claudia Lohff Blatezky. M: Homero Perera	T: (s) F. J. Pagura (e) L. Lythgoe (d) C.L. Blatezky. M: H. Perera	M+T(s) Cancionero Abierto IV (e,d) Worship Book

No.	Writer, translator, composer, arranger	Copyright holder or controller	Source
52	T: (O:e) T. Herbert O'Driscoll (d) D. Trautwein. M: Patrick Wedd	T: (e) Anglican Book Centre, Toronto (d) D. Trautwein. M: Patrick Wedd. Used by permission.	M+T(e) *Alleluia! 20 New Hymns* (d) Worship Book
53	T: (O:e) Fred Kaan (d) D. Trautwein. M: Jamaican folk song, adapted by Doreen Potter	M+T(e) Agápe, Carol Stream, Illinois. Used by permission. (d) D. Trautwein	M+T(e) *Break not the Circle* (d) Worship Book
54	T: (O:swedish) Anders Frostenson (e) David Lewis (d) D. Trautwein (s) P. Sosa. M: Olle Widestrand	M+T(O) Verbum Förlag AB, 12525 Älvsjö, Sweden (e) D. Lewis (d) Burkhardthaus-Laetere Verlag, Gelnhausen (s) P. Sosa. Used by permission.	M+T(O) *Psalmer och Visor 76* (e,s) Worship Book (d) *Frankfurter Lieder*
55	T: (O:russian, +e) Nikolai Zabolotski (d) D. Trautwein. M: Nikolai Zabolotski	M+T(O,e) N. Zabolotski (d) D. Trautwein	Worship Book
56	T: (O:e) T. Herbert O'Driscoll (d) D. Trautwein. M: Henry Hugh Bancroft	T: (e) Anglican Book Centre, Toronto (d) D. Trautwein. M: H.H. Bancroft. Used by permission.	M+T(e) *Alleluia! 20 New Hymns* (d) Worship Book
57	T: (O:quechua, +s) Antonio Morales (e) Eunice L. de Miller (f) E. de Peyer (d) D. Trautwein. M: Antonio Morales	T: (O,s) Centro Andino de Comunicaciones, Cochabamba, Bolivia (e) Mennonite World Conference, Lombard, Illinois. Used by permission. (f) E. de Peyer (d) D. Trautwein	M+T(O,s) *Diosman Taquiycuna, No. 5 del CADEC* (e) *International Songbook* (f,d) Worship Book
58	T: (O:hindi) anonymous (e) Katherine F. Rohrbough (s) P. Sosa. M: Traditional Hindi melody	M+T(O) Jae-Ho, Centenary Music Committee, Lucknow, India (e) Co-operative Recreation Service, Inc., 1958, transferred to World Around Songs, Inc., Burnsville, North Carolina, 1979. Used by permission.	M+T(O,e) *Joyful Songs of India* (s) *Cancionero Abierto III*

59 T: (O:s, +f) from Psalm 144 (145) (e) Eunice L. de Miller (d) Herman Behrend. M: Casiodoro Cardenas

M+T(s) Iglesia del Pacto Evangélico en el Ecuador, Casilla 3327, Quito (e,f,d) Mennonite World Conference, Lombard, Illinois. Used by permission.

M+T(s) Cantad a' Señor Cántico Nuevo (e,f,d) International Songbook

60 T: (O:e) Ronald M. O'Grady (d) D. Trautwein. M: I-to Loh

T(e) R.M. O'Grady (d) D. Trautwein. M: I-to Loh

M+T(e) Hymns from the Four Winds (d) Worship Book

61 T: (O:d) D. Trautwein (e) Fred Kaan. M: D. Trautwein

M+T(d) Burkhardthaus-Laetare Verlag, Gelnhausen (e) Fred Kaan. Used by permission.

M+T(d) Frankfurter Lieder (e) Worship Book

62 T: (O:e) Jane Parker Huber. M: Early American melody

T: (e) Jane Parker Huber

T: (e) Worship Book. M: Lutheran Book of Worship

Sources of illustrations
Sources des illustrations
Quellenangaben für die Illustrationen
Procedencia de las ilustraciones

We wish to thank all those who have granted permission for the use of illustrations in this book. We have made every effort to trace and identify them correctly and to secure all the necessary permissions for reprinting. If we have erred in any way in the acknowledgments, or have unwittingly infringed any copyright, we apologize sincerely. We would be glad to make the necessary corrections in subsequent editions of this book.

Cover: Picture on the theme "Jesus Christ—the Life of the World", based on John 12:24, by Jyoti Sahi, India. In *Und das Wort ist Fleisch geworden,* EOS Druck & Verlag, St Ottilien, FRG, 1976.

Inside cover: Crossing the straits, by Pitseolak. In *Cape Dorset Eskimo Print Calendar 1974,* West Baffin Cooperative Ltd., Cape Dorset, Northwest Territories, Canada, 1973.

Pages xii-xiii: The peacock is a symbol of immortality, the vase a symbol of the water of life. In *The Treasures of Mount Athos,* Ekdotika Athenon SA, Athens, 1973.

Page 2: La vie, by Marc Chagall (286 × 406 cm, huile sur toile, Fondation Maeght, St-Paul-de-Vence, France). 1983, copyright by A.D.A.G.P., Paris and Cosmopress, Geneva.

Page 3: Drawing by Augustin Anaituq.

Page 6: Fowl my friend, by Aloi Piliok. In *Pilioko: Artist of the Pacific,* South Pacific Social Science Association and the Institute of Pacific Studies, University of the South Pacific.

Page 9: "God goes down deep", by Gaumana Gauwrrain. In *Your Kingdom Come: One Month of Meditations on the Lord's Prayer,* CCA, Singapore, 1980.

Page 12: Nativity, by S. E. Bottex, Haiti. By courtesy of CIRIC, Geneva.

Page 16: Pomegranate. In *Coptic Textile Designs,* by M. Gerspach, Dover Publications Inc., New York, 1975.

Page 20: Entombment, by Rosemary Namuli, East Africa. In *Afroasiatische Christliche Kunst,* by Arno Lehmann, Evangelische Verlagsanstalt, Berlin, 1966.

Page 21: The pelican symbolizes Christ's sacrifice on the cross. According to legend, it pierces its breast to feed its offspring with its own blood. In *Seasons and Symbols: a Handbook on the Church Year,* by Robert Wetzler and Helen Huntington, Augsburg, Minneapolis, 1962.

Page 25: "We' re OK. We're waiting for news from you". In *Ismail Schammut,* by Karin Rührdanz, Henschelverlag und Gesellschaft, Berlin, 1975.

Page 29: The five crosses symbolize the five wounds of Christ. In *Armenian Khatch-kars,* Holy See of Etchmiadzin, 1973.

Page 34: The butterfly is a symbol of the resurrection of Christ. In *Grass Roots Art of the Solomons: Images and Islands,* eds John and Sue Chick, Pacific Publications, Sydney and New York, 1978.

Page 42: The cross of the cooperative "La Semilla de Dios", La Palma, El Salvador. Belongs to M. Gilles, YMCA, Geneva.

Page 43: The seven gifts of the Holy Spirit. In *Les Pacificateurs: Jean XXIII, Athénagoras, Paul VI, Dimitrios,* by Aristide Panotis, Edition de la Fondation européenne Dragan, Athens, 1974.

Page 54: Pentecost. In *Watanabe Sadao: Katazome Hanga,* The Logos Church, Robanomimi Publications, Tokyo, 1976.

Page 58: Fish and bread. In *Les Pacificateurs,* by Aristide Panotis, Edition de la Fondation européenne Dragan, Athens, 1974.

Page 62: Hozanna, by John Coburn. In *The Sunburnt Soul: Christianity in Search of an Australian Identity,* by David Millikan, Anzea Publishers, Homebush West, NSW, Australia. Copyright Commonwealth Banking Corp., Sydney.

Page 63: Eucharist symbol. In *Les Pacificateurs,* by Aristide Panotis, Edition de la Fondation européenne Dragan, Athens, 1974.

Page 69: Ears of wheat. In *Les Pacificateurs,* by Aristide Panotis, Edition de la Fondation européenne Dragan, Athens, 1974.

Page 70: Amphora. In *Les symboles dans le Nouveau Testament,* ed. Louis Richard, Geneva, 1960.

Page 72: "Adwoe", symbol of peace. Adinkra symbolism, Ghana.

Page 78: The return of the Prodigal Son, by Rembrandt van Rijn. In *Rembrandt as a Draughtsman,* Phaidon Press Ltd., Oxford and London, 1960.

Page 87: The Tree of Life, 17th century Byzantine icon. By permission of the Greek Orthodox Archdiocese of North and South America.

Page 94: The donkey is a symbol of humility and service. In *Watanabe Sadao: Katazome Hanga,* The Logos Church, Robanomimi Publications, Tokyo, 1976.

Page 104: Two birds. In *Watanabe Sadao: Katazome Hanga,* Vol. 2, The Logos Church, Robanomimi Publications, Tokyo, 1979.

Cover page 3: The raven and the first men, by Bill Reid, Canada. University of British Columbia Museum of Anthropology, Vancouver, Canada.